When Teacher Voices Are Heard

The Future of the Literacy Landscape

Elizabeth Birnam and Debora Nary

ROWMAN & LITTLEFIELD EDUCATION

A division of
ROWMAN & LITTLEFIELD PUBLISHERS, INC.
Lanham • New York • Toronto • Plymouth, UK

KH

To Tate, the anchor that kept my mind focused and my heart believing that I could fulfill a lifelong goal of writing a book. And to the Picarillos, Dubowiks, and Gendreaus, the best team of cheerleaders anyone could ask for!

Much love and appreciation goes out to my brilliant and supportive husband Don; I learn something new from you each and every day. To my kids, Natasha, Maritza and Donny; even when my face is glued to the computer, you are the source of my energy and happiness.

Published by Rowman & Littlefield Education
A division of Rowman & Littlefield Publishers, Inc.
A wholly owned subsidiary of The Rowman & Littlefield Publishing Group, Inc.
4501 Forbes Boulevard, Suite 200, Lanham, Maryland 20706
www.rowman.com

10 Thornbury Road, Plymouth PL6 7PP, United Kingdom

Copyright © 2013 by Elizabeth Birnam and Debora Nary

British Library Cataloguing in Publication Information Available

Library of Congress Cataloging-in-Publication Data Available

Birnam, Elizabeth, 1968–
  When teacher voices are heard : the future of the literacy landscape / Elizabeth Birnam and Debora Nary.
      pages cm
  ISBN 978-1-4758-0074-6 (cloth : alk. paper) — ISBN 978-1-4758-0075-3 (pbk. : alk. paper) — ISBN 978-1-4758-0076-0 (electronic) 1. Literacy—Study and teaching—United States. 2. School improvement programs—United States. I. Nary, Debora, 1962– II. Title.
  LB1576.B4938 2013
  372.6—dc23   2012051241

∞™ The paper used in this publication meets the minimum requirements of American National Standard for Information Sciences—Permanence of Paper for Printed Library Materials, ANSI/NISO Z39.48-1992.

Printed in the United States of America

11/12/13

Contents

Preface

IN DEFENSE OF GOOD TEACHING

Our core premise in writing this book is to share what we observed, experienced, and learned during a curriculum reform undertaking in which a group of teachers refused to be subordinate to curriculum materials. Their passion, knowledge and commitment spawned a literacy reform that no one could have predicted nor believed possible. We will provide a descriptive account of what led up to this reform along with the successes, failures and the roadblocks we faced.

It is our intent to provide the information necessary for other districts to begin their own process of rejuvenating their literacy curricula and as a result, provide their clientele (teachers *and* students) the same opportunity to regain passion for literacy instruction and learning.

This endeavor is neither difficult nor costly and is not reserved just for high-performing schools. This process can be replicated in any district, no matter the size, as long as there is commitment from the teachers and support from the administration. With a little reflection and planning, school districts can create a culture of learning that transforms teachers as well as students. This book is a roadmap to creating reform from the inside out, matching best practices to curriculum standards.

Status Quo: Interrupted

Like many other districts, the district at the heart of this book has a curriculum adoption cycle in which each discipline moves through phases (exploration, implementation, monitoring and evaluation) of review. Significant amounts of money become available for purchase of materials after the exploration phase, so each discipline looks forward to the year they will be able to investigate, ask for, and receive new materials.

Over the years, in the school district that we refer to in our discussion, even though administrators called for coherence, the language arts curriculum became quite convoluted over time. While the administration had purchased a comprehensive K–6 literacy curriculum in 2000, at a cost of over $500,000 for the taxpayers, the three elementary schools and the middle school were using these materials with varying degrees of fidelity. The comprehensive program was seen as adequate and appropriate literature for use as shared reading and guided reading in some schools, while it was held in lesser regard in other buildings.

After the purchase and implementation of this comprehensive program in 2000, two of the elementary schools obtained grants to pursue separate literacy frameworks for instruction. The third elementary school, Main Street, did not have any additional grant money and continued to use the previously purchased program, as did the middle school. The teachers at the grant-receiving buildings became instantaneously enthralled with the framework they were learning about and were vocal about how much professional knowledge they were acquiring and how valuable their new training was to themselves as literacy teachers and to their students. Although this was not the intended result, unfortunately having the three schools trying different processes set up an unhealthy dynamic in the district that would persist for years, ultimately inhibiting the self-efficacy of the teachers at Main Street School, as well as pitting the two grant-receiving schools against each other.

Teachers from all three schools would attend district literacy meetings and Shaw's Lane and Woodlawn teachers would talk enthusiastically about their newly acquired understandings about teaching literacy. As part of their grants, they received additional trainings and materials that were not shared across the district. This set up an "us-against-them" dichotomy where district meetings became ineffective, "an exercise in torture" as more than one teacher phrased it, and where no comprehensive decisions were able to be made.

Approaching the exploration cycle for a new curriculum adoption, the district needed to band together and make common decisions about how to proceed with the request for new materials. The mandate soon came down from the central office that all schools were going to be supplied with identical materials, whatever they may be.

The prior adoption of the comprehensive program had become a fiasco with teachers spending countless hours listening to presentations from sales representatives and piloting materials in their classrooms, only to have the administration veto the teachers' request and purchase a basal program instead.

Teachers were suspicious of the intent of the administration, not comfortable working with each other, and hesitant about putting in the hours and effort it would take to seek out the best language arts materials available. They were certain that the administration would make up their own minds about materials regardless of what the teachers asked for.

Impetus for Change

A representative group from all grade levels across the three elementary schools and the middle school were brought together (under duress) to make a plan of action. The majority of these teachers didn't want to spend time looking at materials because of the history of how curriculum decisions had been made in the past. Others speculated that if they didn't at least look, they really had no basis to complain afterwards.

They decided to start by examining data regarding how each school (on average) was performing on assessment measures. They were hoping to see if there were any common areas of strengths or weaknesses to be able to direct and focus the search for materials. The administration also wanted to highlight the fact that even though two schools had initiated complex staff development programs, student scores were not demonstrating any significant evidence of their success or return on the cost. This tactic, in turn, continued the blame game.

The perception was that the three elementary schools had very different clientele and that no one program could meet the needs of the diverse learners across the three elementary schools: Shaw's Lane, Woodlawn, and Main Street.

Shaw's Lane School is at the end of town where the wealthier neighborhoods are clustered, which includes several waterfront developments. There is strong parent involvement and community support for the school and they are able to have successful fundraisers and initiatives run exclusively by parents. Many Shaw's Lane students have parents that are involved in their education and make sure that homework is done, healthy snacks are packed, and their children have experiences that support oral language development and complex understandings. Over the years, Shaw's Lane School earned the reputation of being the "Country Day School."

Conversely, the neighborhood that encompasses Woodlawn School includes a substantive subsidized housing complex and consequently the socioeconomic average of its student population is much lower, with a high number of free and reduced lunch recipients. This percentage qualifies the school as a "school wide" assistance Title I participant and brings in substantial funding annually to Woodlawn School alone. Woodlawn uses this money for books, training, and (most coveted) personnel to help address the additional needs of their population. The needs of this population are indeed vast, with the average first grader beginning formal education scoring two to three years below expected on measures of literacy acquisition.

The population of Main Street School ranges somewhere between that of Shaw's Lane and Woodlawn. Main Street has a percentage of free and reduced lunch candidates around 45 percent, which is close to, but just barely out of reach for federal assistance. Main Street School serves working families where both parents are employed and have limited time to volunteer and help with homework and special projects.

Main Street also has a much higher percentage of diverse cultures of students qualifying for English for Speakers of Other Languages services. These students and their families need help learning the language, as well as assistance in negotiating the American culture. In addition, Main Street School also has a small number of upper-class neighborhoods which sets up an interesting dichotomy: children who are privileged and children who are not. On assessment measures, Main Street students typically score very high or very low, with a modest number of students in the middle range.

Students from these three elementary schools, all with different cultures, training, and experience, feed into the middle school. Administration was facing an uphill battle. How were all design-team members going to agree on a literacy curriculum? Would it even be possible to work together?

Fast forward one year later. This story has a happy and extremely successful ending. The teachers of this district were granted permission to write their own literacy curriculum. Its birth and early evolution were not pretty. In fact, some might say it was one of the most frustrating years of their teaching careers; however, the results have proven the worth of their blood, sweat, and tears. Test scores have increased dramatically and the literacy growth of the students across the district is remarkable.

Upon analyzing data by way of a growth model that looks at the change in a student's achievement over at least two points in time as compared to the student's peers, it was found that students at the middle school achieved statistically significant growth in reading since the implementation of the new home-grown reading program. In fact, the growth was rated "high" on state measures.

In data analysis, proficiency reflects what the student brings to school, while, in contrast, measures of growth reflect what school adds to the student. A consultant hired to analyze the data concluded that the growth of the middle school students was likely due to a program responsive to the needs of students and would have been difficult to achieve from a packaged program.

This is not a book about curriculum or professional development; rather this book is about the kind of grassroots reform that can happen when teachers' voices are heard and the knowledge and professionalism of the collective are respected. This is a book about what the future of the literacy landscape in America could be: A place where students and teachers alike are passionate about reading and writing and where parents and administrators are thrilled with the achievement growth of their students.

Acknowledgments

We began exploring and experimenting with ways in which literacy could be reformed in our school district. Over time, we realized how the process transformed us personally and professionally. By writing this book, we were able to share our experience and all that we learned. We have many people to thank.

First and foremost is Jean Briggs-Badger. As our curriculum coordinator at the onset of the project and now our unstoppable superintendent, Jean was the catalyst that moved a mere idea into actual conception, and eventually a reality. Her unwavering belief in the teachers of Dover inspired them to go beyond the classroom walls as she challenged them to become leaders in literacy. They never let her down.

We thank all of the teachers who were and continue to be a part of the Dover Literacy Team. They are truly outstanding educators. Without them and their undying dedication, the strides made across the district could have never happened. The children of Dover will always be indebted to you.

We thank:

Jackie Tromba and Paula Glynn, two members of the design team whose knowledge of literacy has been invaluable. Jackie, an indisputable expert in all things having to do with literacy and Paula, a natural at project management, made the implementation of the program as seamless as possible.

The principals of the Dover school district who dealt with and continue to understand the potential uncertainties that arise with a home-grown curriculum. Their flexibility and risk taking have not gone unnoticed.

Todd DeMitchell—a professor, published author many times over, and one of the most intelligent, down-to-earth guys we have ever met. Thank you for your consultation and enthusiastic support of our endeavor.

Thanks also to Dr. John O'Connor, former Superintendent of Schools, who had faith in the skill and tenacity of teachers in his district.

Professionally, there are far too many people to recognize. We are fortunate to have had the experiences along the way that helped shape us into the educators we are today.

Introduction

Thoughtfully adaptive teachers get the best results. The new laws are not designed to encourage teachers to use professional judgment; on the contrary, they are designed to ensure compliance with a "perfect method."

—Duffy & Hoffman (1999)

IMAGINE

Imagine if you will two school systems well into the early twenty-first century. Both systems have dedicated teachers who are motivated to make a difference in the lives of their students. Both systems, although not wealthy, have enough resources to adequately outfit classrooms with materials and supplies.

Families serviced by these systems run the gamut of linguistic, cultural, and educational backgrounds and this diversity encompasses families who receive free and reduced lunch, families who are new to the United States as well as those who enjoy robust educational and experiential encounters outside of school. Most notably, both of these systems, like countless others across the nation, have teetered on the brink of failing to make adequate yearly progress (AYP) specified by the No Child Left Behind Act for the past few years and have recently succumbed to the proclamation that they are "A District In Need of Improvement" (DINI).

Although similar in many ways up to this point, the individual path each of these districts takes in response to the unenviable DINI status is radically different.

School District #1

The administration and school board of District #1 assume that teachers have been doing their best to bring scores up and meet the needs of their diverse student body but did not produce the results they all hoped and needed to attain. They recognize that their teachers need help. What they have been doing for years is clearly not working any longer and with the standards consistently on the increase, changes need to be put in place.

Publishing companies have stepped up to the plate to address this growing need for school districts to improve literacy instruction results through producing "core curricula" (literacy programs that are all inclusive; containing reading, writing, spelling, and grammar instruction) that claim to be "scientifically based."

The core curricula use as their foundation the five pillars of reading instruction detailed by the National Reading Panel's 2000 report on reading instruction in America. Because of the claims of success these off-the-shelf literacy programs tout and the perceived ease of implementation, these core programs have been widely adopted by school administrators, politicians, and even some educators, who are struggling with how best to improve the reading and writing abilities of their students.

The curriculum coordinator of District #1 approaches this problem by investigating the publisher-produced integrated programs. Because there are only four major literacy curriculum publishing houses (Pearson, McGraw-Hill, Houghton Mifflin [which encompasses Harcourt], and Scholastic), this is not a time-consuming or drawn-out task. She narrows down the initial search to the three top-selling curricula, which boast an increase in student achievement for school departments who fully implement the program as directed. The curriculum coordinator forms a committee of interested teachers to listen to the sales presentations and to pilot these programs.

Teachers initially enthusiastically embrace these programs in the hopes of securing a better learning experience for their students. They listen eagerly to the presenters who promise great success for their students if they systematically follow the curriculum scope and sequence and do not deviate from the curriculum design.

After only a short while, some teachers realize that, although their average-achieving students are progressing in their literacy acquisition as advertised, students who have special needs were not getting everything they need. For example, time to read books of the students' own choosing at the appropriate independent and instructional levels was difficult to find in the scripted curriculum.

This is especially true for those students who struggle, as they are targeted for intervention work that constricts flexibility. Unfortunately, many of these students who need time for pleasure reading actually receive less of an opportunity for this important activity in most classrooms.

Teachers in School District #1 soon realize that they cannot continue the strict adherence to the scope and sequence of the newly adopted literacy program. However, because of the administration's concern with raising student scores and their adherence to the publishing company's admonishment that results cannot be guaranteed if teachers deviate from the units as written, teachers in District #1 avoid revealing to the administration, and sometimes to each other, that they are indeed supplementing the program.

Not only are these teachers dissatisfied with the literacy experiences they are providing their students, some argue that these experiences are "miseducative"—a term John Dewey used over fifty years ago to describe a situation in which the learning experience is negative and in fact, produces an experience that hinders the intellectual growth of the individual (Dewey, 1939).

These dissatisfied but caring teachers know that they are making defensible decisions regarding student literacy progress and language acquisition, but they are not sure they can articulate, or even want to try to explain their reasons for veering from the basalization/standardization culture that was established by their well-meaning administrators who also want the best for their students.

The teachers who tried to implement the curriculum with the fidelity of adherence with no deviation or substitution required in the program do not find the curriculum any more professionally satisfying. They find the endless "activities" a bit overwhelming when trying to select the most effective lessons for their students.

These educators guide their weekly planning by what the curriculum guide outlines and do not seek out alternative methods. If it is not in the teacher's guide, it must not be appropriate for these students at this time of year, they think. These teachers quickly become disillusioned about their efficacy as literacy teachers as they relinquish their instructional decision making to the program.

Their sense of standing as professionals who make informed decisions based on the existing research is compromised. When adopting a packaged literacy curriculum, the trade-off involves the substitution of the value of efficiency (cost effective in terms of time expended to find the best curriculum) for the value of excellence gained through the application of child-centered curriculum and research expertise.

Pre-packaged curricula reduce the opportunity for reading teachers and curriculum specialists to know what is happening out there in the "research world." Spending time in that world builds skills and knowledge central to work of the education profession in general and to reading teachers specifically.

School District #2

The administrators in School District #2 initially approach the wilting standardized scores in the same manner as School District #1. They also assume that their teachers are doing the absolute best job that they can and they are perplexed as to why scores remain stagnant or had declined in places. Their student body had become more and more diverse over the years but they had established supports for those students. They too, invited in a variety of reading programs for their teachers to consider.

While both school districts used the same initial strategy, School District #2 took a different path at a critical juncture in the process. When the teachers balked at the scripted curriculum under review and questioned the lesson plans that were labeled "differentiated," the administrators listened. They paid attention when the teachers described the kinds of differentiation they were already providing for the most diverse students in their classrooms.

Administrators were intent on understanding how precisely teachers were assessing the learning level each individual student and how they tailored lessons that specifically address those students' weaknesses while supporting their strengths. They recognized the passion in the teachers' voices as they articulated how they coordinate existing curriculum that reflects the state standards, while being responsive to each student's unique interests and reading level. Administrators knew they were hearing the voices of their most passionate literacy teachers. They also recognized that not all teachers were in the same place.

Both the administration and the teachers were now at an impasse. The teachers do not want to be required to teach from a basal. They are familiar with the research that indicates the gradual de-professionalism of teachers who use basals. They are fiercely protective of their own autonomy and decision-making responsibilities for the students in their classes. They are worried about having a curriculum that specifies "if it's Tuesday, October 14th, you're on page 83."

Conversely, administrators are in the unenviable positions of having their schools in jeopardy of "restructuring," ultimately resulting in the dismissal of the principal if scores do not improve. They are hesitant to give up their assumptions and faith in the great success stories that the publishing companies tout regarding these curricular programs. After all, these programs offer a level of comfort knowing that they had been effective in other struggling districts.

School District #2 is at a crossroads. The administrators have invested in the core basal reading program. They have listened to the teachers who have voiced strong opposition to the wholesale implementation of the reading program. But what to do?

Ultimately, as the district recognized the extraordinary influence teachers have on the achievement of students, it was time to end the impasse. Although facing possible sanctions through No Child Left Behind DINI procedures, these administrators were not willing to squander the wealth of knowledge and expertise their teachers bring to their work in favor of a curriculum-in-a-box. As the administration and teacher-leaders came together to generate ideas on how to deal with the curriculum issue, a powerful and empowering idea began to take shape.

They realized they possessed the knowledge, skill and desire to create their own literacy curriculum! Publishing houses do not own the research and they are not the only experts in education. Teachers and administrators who are educated, experienced, and highly knowledgeable of their community and their students can step up to the challenge. A decision was made to build on and rely on the expertise that already existed in the school district. The experts were not outside the school district; they were already in the school district. This leap of faith offered great rewards but also offered great challenges.

Over the course of two years, and with an equal dose of support and pressure from the administration, a committed group of teachers took matters into their own hands, eventually creating a curriculum, with many unintended, yet positive, consequences, which all stakeholders viewed with pride.

Reflecting on the process and outcome, it is easy for them to see that teachers appreciate working collaboratively, while retaining their individual professional decision-making capabilities. The teachers found a renewed sense of enthusiasm and motivation for providing an intensive and a responsive curriculum in which all of their students receive what they need in order to move forward in literacy acquisition.

Administrators gained a deep respect for the accomplishments of the teachers, as well as the professional development the teachers provided to their principals. The administration more clearly recognized the issues facing literacy learners. Students and parents were thrilled that every child was receiving reading instruction at her individual learning level and was receiving appropriate supports and challenges for continuous learning.

Students were able to engage in reading activities for extended periods and had time to talk about books and authors with their classmates. Parents reported visiting the library more often at the request of their children and saw more authentic reading at home. Student literacy scores improved, student enjoyment of reading improved, and parental satisfaction with their children's skills and abilities grew.

Which school district would you prefer to have your child attend? For which school district would *you* like to work?

Although they are examples of challenges faced by school districts, the dilemmas portrayed in these two vignettes are playing out across the nation. More often than not, the tale of School District #1 has been the typical response to the challenge to raise literacy scores; however, the response from School District #2 is the more robust option for teachers, students, and their families.

School District #2 embraces a capacity-building strategy that calls on the expertise of its teachers while at the same time building the expertise of those teachers. The response to the mandate to improve student scores was met with a strategy of building capacity within the teaching ranks.

Fortunately, School District #2 is not a hypothetical place, but an actual school district where teachers are efficacious and administration honors and trusts their commitment and drive. Though not always the case, these professionals have recently taken great pains to establish a culture of learning, sharing with consistent reflection on teaching methods in order to provide the best possible education for students of a variety of cultural, ethnic, linguistic, educational, and socioeconomical backgrounds—students who represent the future of our country.

This book will offer a descriptive account of what can happen in a school district that honors the professional knowledge of teachers, respects their ability to be responsive to their students, and designs instruction that meets and exceeds the standards. It will expose and analyze underlying problems that can emerge when diverse adults try to collaborate about something as potentially personal as literacy instruction. We will detail and expand upon a process of literacy reform proven successful in more ways than in just achievement scores.

Every chapter in this book opens with a "snapshot" of the successes and challenges teachers and literacy leaders in a midsize New England school district faced during each stage in the reform process. We hope this will offer a realistic, albeit sometimes humorous, look at the implementation of this reform project. Additionally, each chapter ends with a summary of the most critical points.

Chapter 1 describes the visioning stage of considering a district-wide literacy reform. It details the work that needs to happen by the administration and literacy leaders to set the stage for the teachers' work. Literacy reform initiatives are intensive and can become frustrating for teachers if the vision is not there. Teachers want to know that their efforts will manifest in a better learning environment for their students, their colleagues, and themselves. The visioning stage is crucial in laying the groundwork for the future of this reform.

Chapter 2 illustrates the design of this literacy reform. Readers become acquainted with how teaching philosophies and best practices in the pedagogy of literacy can be crafted into a framework for successful instruction.

Chapter 3 consists of a variety of templates and forms demonstrating one way a home-grown literacy curriculum can be designed. Components are broken down and detailed. Lesson plan formats, outlines, and assessment procedures are included. Chapter 3 also includes a sample scope and sequence, and the breakdown of how to write and implement a responsive focus lesson, as well as tips on maximizing the literacy block. Attention is also paid to vocabulary instruction and word study and their place in the workshop.

Very few, if any, educational innovations are implemented without support of the teachers on the ground floor. In chapter 4, we investigate the importance of instituting supportive measures to assist teachers in this endeavor. Consideration is paid to establishing methods of collaboration between teachers and administrators and the introduction of the position of literacy facilitator will be discussed. The literacy facilitator's responsibilities include supporting curriculum design, delivering job-embedded professional development, and overseeing district-wide communication and consistency between all of the schools in the district.

Chapter 5 will illustrate the various ways in which a district can tap into its very own resources in order to establish and encourage professional development within and across schools. This chapter focuses on ideal ways to provide professional development for teachers that allows them to conceptualize and create a literacy curriculum.

The professional development described here is not costly, yet has long-term impact and transformative power on a teacher's practice. We take current research on teacher knowledge and decision making and illustrate how that can be applied in districts of any size. Examples of how classroom teachers, reading specialists, and literacy facilitators provide continuous job-embedded professional development when it's needed and to those who need/ want it are provided.

Chapter 6 takes on the issue of differentiation to meet the needs of all students. We know that all learners do not respond to the same instruction in the same ways. This chapter explains how differentiation is handled in a home-grown curriculum and how teachers target the learning needs of all students while affording them the most appropriate materials on which to practice.

The final chapter, chapter 7, tackles the notion of how to determine whether or not a home-grown, teacher-created program is having an effect on student growth. It is no surprise in this age of accountability that administrators and literacy leaders are not willing to wait years or even months to discover what is working well and what is not. Methods of immediate feedback are built into this type of reform and this chapter will alert the decision makers on how, where, and when to look for authentic and quality feedback. Templates for data collection are embedded in this chapter.

The book ends with questions and answers that we grappled with all along the reform process.

The teachers in the highlighted district are more than teachers; they are writers, artists, philosophers, and leaders. As seen in the snapshots at the beginning of every chapter, they proved to their administrators and the community that their capabilities surpassed the expectations anyone had for them. Through the process literacy instruction was reformed for teachers and refined for the students. This is a story with a happy ending. It shows that reading reform can be successfully created from the bottom up and have a lasting and transformational effect on the students and teachers of the district.

Chapter One

The Visioning Stage

SNAPSHOT #1

It is a sweltering one hundred degrees on this late June morning and school was dismissed for summer break two days ago; however, more than sixty teachers still remain on campus, huddled over laptops, reassembling notebooks and debating the match between state standards and lesson objectives. There is no air-conditioning, no ceiling fan, nor any students, but this doesn't faze these professionals; they are serious about their mission and will stop at nothing to develop top quality lessons for the district literacy program.

While most teachers are devoted, hard working, and diligent, the level of commitment exuded by teachers of this middle-class community exceeds all expectations. This district began a journey into reforming literacy instruction that would force teachers to make hard decisions, clarify and stand their ground on personal philosophies of literacy instruction, and dive into professional development to a level previously unheard of in many school districts. This is a David and Goliath story detailing one teaching staff's fight for best practices and common sense instruction in literacy. They were up against a wave of low standardized test scores, administrator panic about those scores, and current politics over effective curriculum.

Faced with a new literacy curriculum adoption, teachers in this town faced some formidable opponents: the administration and the school board. Publication of their previously adopted core curriculum had been stopped and the district was preparing a budget request for the new curriculum cycle to purchase a new literacy curriculum. District leaders assembled a team of teachers across the city's three elementary schools and the middle school and charged this group with selecting the best literacy curriculum for their students.

At first, this group proceeded in typical fashion. They requested and received copies of several core curricula available on the educational market. Representatives from publishing companies supplied free tee-shirts and book bags filled with school supplies and candy to these teachers along with their presentations. Their PowerPoints contained everything a seasoned educator would expect—connections to research, ample teaching ideas, and a wealth of assessment promises. Teachers at each building teamed up to "pilot" these programs.

So far, there is nothing unusual about this adoption process; schools and districts follow similar procedures every year when choosing new programs. What soon began to happen, however, was unexpected, unprecedented and unnerving to all involved.

THE EVOLVING LITERACY LANDSCAPE

Over the past decade, three issues have taken hold of literacy education to influence how instruction is perceived and carried out by teachers, parents, administrators, and politicians. These issues are:

1. The evolution of the standards movement.
2. The report of the National Reading Panel.
3. The reliance on scientifically based literacy instruction (Shannon, in Kucer 2008, p. 3–16).

Unfortunately, these issues have had the capacity to limit the autonomous decision making of teachers and to sever opportunities for differentiation of instruction.

Billions of dollars each year are spent on literacy education in our public schools, yet stories of illiteracy, alliteracy, and sanctions against underperformance of the reading and writing ability of American students (as compared to students across the globe) are rampant in the media. Newspaper articles highlight "failing schools" while providing "Annual Yearly Progress" levels to the public, many of whom may not understand the ramifications or the complexity of such reporting of scores. In response, school governing boards and administrators are faced with the choice of either defending the literacy curriculum they have in place, or seeking out an alternative magic bullet curriculum that claims results in student achievement.

Publishing companies have responded by developing curricular programs that are portable across school districts without regard for student and community factors. In essence, the publishers have developed programs that have a cookie-cutter quality to them, which reduces professional decision making to a technical activity that the teacher implements in the prescribed manner. In many ways, these programs reduce the messiness and complexity of teaching and learning to preferred algorithms. The concept, "if you follow the teachers guide you are a fail-proof teacher," is not the reality of teaching that we have lived. There is another way.

Current literacy core programs are highly scripted curricula where the role of the teacher in curriculum implementation is to read the script and ensure that students are engaged and moving through the steps. These curricula are built on the belief that students learn to read by decoding words and building sight word vocabularies, thus increasing reading fluency. Once rapid recognition of large banks of sight words is mastered, it is assumed that comprehension will be automatic.

These types of highly scripted programs have several benefits for teachers and administration. A few are:

- Planning on the teacher's part has already been done and the sight words, stories and skills have been matched and aligned with one another.
- Consistency across classrooms and school systems—all students are guaranteed the same opportunities/materials.
- Scope and sequence is laid out and is made available to the public.

However, there are serious potential drawbacks from implementing a highly scripted curriculum:

- All students do not learn the same way.
- This script doesn't allow for teacher flexibility in accommodating diverse learners.
- Research consistently demonstrates that the teacher is the most important variable in student learning—not the curriculum materials. Scripted programs tie the teacher's hands in making instructional decisions that are responsive to student needs and contribute to "de-skilling" teachers.
- Research demonstrates that these types of highly scripted programs that are tightly tied to phonetic acquisition and word identification are relatively successful in teaching children how to decode words, but are not as strong at bringing about higher-level comprehension (Gamse, Jacob, Horst, Boulay, & Unlu 2008, p. v).

These core programs insist that student achievement will be compromised unless teachers maintain fidelity to the script, thus increasing the fervor of administration to dissuade teachers from veering away from the script (Diamond 2004, p. 1–3).

Because of the sheer volume of research collected and provided by publishing companies, it is difficult for a single district to pinpoint and recognize alternative hypotheses to explain the increase in student improvement in response to using a basal or "core" literacy curriculum. In such cases, school boards, administrators and even teachers begin to be convinced that core literacy programs are the holy grail of education and will be able to reach students in all of their diversity while ensuring positive results.

These changes have impacted teachers and curricula in significant ways. Many educators have become disillusioned about their efficacy as literacy teachers and the value of their instructional methods. Not only are teachers dissatisfied with the literacy experiences they are providing for their students, some may even argue that these experiences are "miseducative."

DEFINING REFORM

The dictionary defines reform in its verb form as "improving something by removing faults." As a noun, it states it as "reorganization and improvement." One question that undergirds the concept of reform is: what are the reasons that shape the need for the reformation? In addition, who are the integral players in the change process and how do they instill the need for change among their peers who may not see the need for or are reluctant to change?

To many in the field of education as well as the stakeholders affected by it, reform may be synonymous with contention. Many try to avoid it while others who understand its value and place in education stay silent, so as not to disrupt the status quo. In Amy Gutman's book *Democratic Education* (1987), she explores the concept of democracy's role in the shaping of American education. She explains the need for the sometimes contentious political discourse and controversy if change is to occur. She makes a direct connection to social progress and education.

Gutman asserts that it has become commonplace to "neglect educational alternatives that may be better than those to which we have become accustomed or that may aid us in understanding how to improve our schools before we reach a point of crisis, when our reactions are likely to be less reflective because we have so little time to deliberate" (Gutman 1987, p. 88). For progressive educators who have been in the field long enough, this ideological thinking illustrates their frustration.

This call for reform is not new. More than twenty years ago, Brenda Hawkins from the Jamestown Education Foundation wrote "as our nation's population continues to grow and become increasingly diverse, schools must change to meet the needs and demands of an increasingly multicultural, multilingual, and global society. The challenges to be faced in the future will not be met by individuals who learn skills designed for the past in schools today" (in Kucer 2008, p. 250). Since then, there has been little headway in improving the literacy achievement of American students.

Change continues to be a necessity if we are to prepare children for the demands of a competitive society.

Despite the dire need for reform, the area of literacy instruction has been slow to change over the last eighty to ninety years. Oftentimes, when reading instruction reform *does* take place it is accomplished in a localized manner and through clandestine means. Conscientious teachers recognize when an approach they are using proves unfruitful. They take it upon themselves to adjust instruction within the confines of their own classroom.

Although these individuals realize change is vital system-wide, they feel powerless, so they direct their energy where they know they can make a difference. Being creative and passionate human beings, it is not unusual for teachers to take this subversive approach rather than wait for the decision makers in the school district who are seeking a "miracle" program that will elevate test scores and "fix" the problem. Innovative teachers will not waste any time; they will work their "magic" on their own terms and usually at the expense of their own bank accounts.

Educators are visionaries but literacy reform must not stop at the classroom door. It takes a perfect storm of open-minded administrators and vocal teachers to work together to find the ways and means necessary to provide reading instruction that is holistic and mindful of their student population. Context for instruction is important.

One option is to look beyond the prepackaged, commercial programs and to dig deep inside and capitalize on this creativity and passion by utilizing the human resources in the school district. Careful collaboration can create systematic, dynamic reform in literacy instruction that meets the specific needs of the students, targets the standards, and fosters the creativity and autonomy of the teachers who implement it. A teacher-created program does this. It respects the professional knowledge of educators and takes into account the individuality of each student, while aligning content to state and national standards.

LAYING THE FOUNDATION: THE WORK BEFORE THE WORK

Establishing a Visionary Mindset

Many would agree that change is frightening. It can bring out the best in us, as well as the worst. Inarguably, whenever a group of people embarks on a high-stakes project requiring a large amount of creative energy, personality idiosyncrasies, and even egos, can prove to be seemingly immovable obstacles. Often, a period of time may be required to understand one another and to accept differences before the creative process can begin to take shape. Many professionals are passionate about their practice and believe that the approach they have taken to meet a set of objectives is irrefutable; so why change it?

Just as trends in science and technology constantly evolve over time, so should a literacy curriculum. A malleable curriculum allows teachers to be better able to provide their students with lessons that are relevant, while targeting and making use of contemporary resources.

Expecting the school and curriculum to change based on the needs of its students is the foundation of *transformative* education influenced by the social change agenda that Michael Apple (1994) wrote about. "Transformative educators believe that the school should fit a child, rather than expecting the child to conform to school regimentation (Hawkins in Kucer, 2008). This philosophy is the basis of a literacy program produced by the teachers who will teach it.

If literacy instruction is to be reformed by way of a teacher-created, homegrown program, it requires all members of its design team to be visionaries as they navigate their way through the ever-changing and sometimes turbulent waters of education.

It necessitates teacher involvement since they are the people most closely connected to the children. In this democratic model, classroom teachers do not sit by idly, merely waiting for the administration to make arbitrary, systematic changes to the curriculum that may or may not improve their instruction and their students' learning. Instead, systemic changes are the result of a participatory approach (Gutman, 1999) where all of the district's practitioners are invited and encouraged to contribute to their students' learning.

Just as forward-thinking educators find teaching to be ineffective when a disciplinary approach is used on their students, progressive, reform-minded administrators are willing to incorporate the expertise of their staff members in the process of redefining effective literacy instruction, rather than imposing a curriculum they do not believe in and managing its implementation with sticks and carrots. This approach inculcates an investment in all students' success and is the ideology on which a home-grown literacy program is founded.

Teachers creating a literacy program that fits the needs of their students must know where they are and where they want to be before they can write the roadmap that will lead them to their objective. Conversely, a commercial, core program has already made that determination. It therefore requires children to follow a predetermined pathway regardless of their prior experiences and future needs. Teachers feel marginalized, as if their knowledge of student learning is irrelevant, rather than inspired to build upon what their students bring to the classroom and contribute to the curriculum. This attitude of ineffectiveness, simply put, is the obstacle that will ultimately thwart student success.

However, if a group of teachers feels that the expertise they bring to the school is valued and they are encouraged to share their knowledge, their perceptions of student success is the driving force within a curriculum. They can envision student achievement.

Through this notion of collective teacher efficacy, teachers truly believe that they have the necessary skills for positive student outcomes and can effectively prepare their students to be active participants in the world around them (Brinson and Steiner, 2007). In a teacher-created literacy program, the heart of the program is the teachers who create it, teach it, and regularly modify it. In order for the program to work, every professional in the building is asked to participate in any capacity, so it only makes sense that through varying degrees of participation, a sense of efficacy is born that is able to sustain itself throughout the years.

With this attitude, instruction becomes a transparent and communal process. This is a radical shift in the age-old belief that teaching is an isolated profession. A transparent attitude toward teaching hints that districts can avoid what Common (1983) deemed as the "power of the doorknob." Doorknobs have wielded great power in the history of education, in that teachers can close their classroom doors and teach the way they think is best for their students no matter what curriculum is used or what mandates are handed down.

The power of the doorknob is often evoked when a district adopts a pre-packaged, core program to the dismay of its teachers. Once the classroom door is closed, teachers revert to the way they believe their students *should* learn, not what the administration *mandates* they teach.

In a home-grown program, teacher ownership becomes the driving force for its success. Classroom doors are open as teacher investment in the program creates a desire to learn from one another and implement instructional techniques with consistency, and fidelity to ensure that standards and skills are covered in their entirety. To a teacher invested in the design and implementation of a home-grown program, poor scores and failing students could potentially signal to nervous administrators that the program should be replaced with a packaged curriculum that runs counter to the pedagogical philosophy of these progressive teachers.

Teachers will be quick to re-evaluate their path of instruction and to seek assistance with any roadblocks to student learning. Intrinsic motivation is built in as teachers fear having their reinvigorated professionalism reduced.

Establishing Powerful and Reinforcing Growth Potentials

The long-term goal of creating a teacher-designed curriculum may be over-whelming to consider at the outset. As with all large projects, small achievements sustain the work and motivation necessary for participants to continue their commitment. The same holds true for curriculum change. In attempting an endeavor this comprehensive, it is helpful to consider the words of Peter Senge, a pioneer in the field of management innovation, when he compares growing an innovative idea to growing a tree:

> The seed contains the possibilities for a tree, but it realizes that possibility through an emergent reinforcing growth process. The seed sends out small feelers. These primitive roots draw in more water and nutrients, and so on. The initial growth process is under way. But how far it progresses depends on a host of limits: water, nutrients in the soil, space for the roots to expand, warmth. Eventually, as the tree begins to extend beyond the surface, other limits will come into play: sunlight, space for the tree's branches to spread, insects that will destroy the tree's leaves. (Senge 1999, p. 8)

Keeping this in mind, a crucial first task for a project manager of this type of curriculum endeavor is to be aware of and understand the reinforcements to innovative growth as well as possible limitations. These reinforcements will contribute to, and sustain, positive movement when roadblocks arise. Any long-term innovation will struggle to sustain positive momentum, and unless the balance between forward movement and roadblocks is maintained, there is potential for the inevitable roadblocks to halt or prematurely end the growth. Resiliency will prevail if participants have encountered sufficient powerful reinforcing growth experiences.

Designing the Work Teams: It's All about Disposition

Throughout this endeavor, but especially at the outset, it is critical for the facilitator or manager of the project to gather passionate, motivated, and optimistic teacher-leaders who appreciate the restraints a core curriculum will put on their ability to make responsive instructional decisions: decisions based on their knowledge of best practices and the students in their classrooms. They must be strong teachers who appreciate their own ability to effect the achievement of their students. In other words, they must be efficacious.

Yet, narcissism should not be confused with passion. Not only do these initial teachers need to be efficacious themselves, but they also need to be open-minded enough to recognize and admit that what has always worked for them in the past may not work for everyone and there may be other ways of approaching teaching challenges.

As we will discuss shortly, a robust respect for the teaching practices of their colleagues will also be critical.

Though they may be strong and driven, these teachers will not be able to jump immediately into designing a literacy curriculum; on the contrary, they will need time and opportunity to become a learning community with one another. As with any seed, a true bottom-up approach grows slowly over time and flourishes on consistent nurturing.

Sparking Positive Momentum through Knowledge

Indoctrination will most surely lead to failure. Instead, the goal is for teachers to construct their own opinions about the effects of core curricula and, through social interaction, come to the realization that, as a team, they possess the knowledge and skills necessary to recognize best practices in literacy instruction and to assimilate those best practices into their teaching repertoire.

This initial group, commonly referred to in schools and business as a "task force" or "pilot group" as we will call it, will require access to background information and research on core curricula and teacher quality. The first few organizational meetings should encompass readings and discussions juxtaposing the effects of core curricula and professional teacher quality on instructional decision-making capabilities. Examples of quality readings are in table 1.1.

Opportunity for collaboration and reflection will reinforce the commitment of individual members of this pilot group. As they share teaching methods, coach each other in learning new methods, and experience personal professional growth, they become aware of the satisfaction of opening their classroom doors to colleagues and being invited in to observe another teacher's practice. This phase in the "work before the work" is crucial for teachers to realize that they are more alike than they previously may have thought. While they may have different terms for practices, in reality the techniques are strikingly similar. This realization will lead to the necessary reinforcement of collective efficacy.

The Importance of Efficacy

"Believe it and you will achieve it" is a mantra that helps individuals reach personal goals. In social cognitive theory, this phenomenon is referred to as "self-efficacy" (Bandura 1986, 1997). Self-efficacy is an individual's belief about her or his capacity to pursue and execute actions that will lead to successful achievement of a goal.

Table 1.1. Professional Resources to Guide Teacher Decision Making

Achinstein, B., & Ogawa, R. T. (2006). (In) Fidelity: What the resistance of new teachers reveals about professional principles and prescriptive educational policies. *Harvard Educational Review*, 76(1), 30–63.

Allington, R. (2001). *What really matters for struggling readers*. New York: Longman.

Dudley-Marling, C., & Paugh, P. (2005). The rich get richer; The poor get direct instruction. In B. Altwerger (Ed.), *Reading for profit: How the bottom line leaves kids behind* (pp. 156–171). Portsmouth, NH: Heinemann.

Duncan-Owens, D. (2009). Scripted reading programs: Fishing for success. *Principal*, 88, 26–29.

Fang, Z., Fu, D., & Lamme, L. L. (2004). From scripted instruction to teacher empowerment: Supporting literacy teachers to make pedagogical transitions. *Literacy*, 35(1), 58–64.

Gerstl-Pepin, C. I., & Woodside-Jiron, H. (2005). Tensions between the "science" of reading and a "love of learning": One high-poverty school's struggle with NCLB. *Equity and Excellence in Education*, 38(3), 232–41.

Hargreaves, A., & Fullan, M. (2012). *Professional capital: transforming teaching in every school*. New York: Teachers College Press .

Hassett, D. D. (2008). Teacher flexibility and judgment: A multidynamic literacy theory. *Journal of Early Childhood Literacy*, 8(3), 295–327.

Ingersoll, R. M. (2003). Who controls teachers' work?: *Power and accountability in America's schools*. Cambridge: Harvard University Press.

Joseph, R. (2006). "I won't stop what I'm doing": The factors that contribute to teachers' proactive resistance to scripted literacy programs. Paper presented at the annual meeting of the American Educational Research Association.

MacGillivray, L., Ardell, A. L., Curwen, M. S., & Palma, J. (2004). Colonized teachers: Examining the implementation of a scripted reading program. *Teaching Education*, 15(2), 131–44.

McCarthey, S. (2008). The impact of No Child Left Behind on teachers' writing instruction. Written Communication, 25(4), 462–505.

McGill-Franzen, A., Zmach, C., Solic, K., & Zeig, J. L. (2006). The confluence of two policy mandates: Core reading programs and third-grade retention in Florida. *The Elementary School Journal*, 107(1), 67–91.

Moustafa, M., & Land, R. E. (2002). The reading achievement of economically disadvantaged children in urban schools using Open Court vs. comparably disadvantaged children in urban schools using nonscripted reading programs. In *Yearbook of Urban Learning, Teaching, and Research*. Special Interest Group of the American Educational Research Association, pp. 44–53.

Pease-Alvarez, L., & Samway, K. D. (2008). Negotiating a top-down reading program mandate: The experience of one school. *Language Arts*, 86(1), 32–41.

Reeves, J. (2010). Teacher learning by script. *Language Teaching Research* 14: 241–58.

Smagorinsky, P. (2009). The cultural practice of reading and the standardized assessment of reading instruction: When incommensurate worlds collide. *Educational Researcher*, 38(7), 522–27.

Wilson, P., Martens, P., Arya, P., & Altwerger, B. (2004). Readers, instruction, and the NRP. *Phi Delta Kappan*, 86(3), 242–246.

The strength of one's self-efficacy beliefs affects the level of motivation, intention, and amount of effort one puts into achieving goals. If one's self-efficacy is low, that individual is more likely to become easily frustrated and give up on goals. In contrast, if one's self-efficacy is high, that individual will display resiliency despite setbacks and persist through roadblocks on the way to achieving a goal.

Teacher self-efficacy refers to one's own ability to affect student achievement. A teacher who has high teacher-efficacy has the expectation that she will able to reach all students and provide them with a learning environment that allows them to be successful learners.

Research suggests that high efficacy teachers are more likely to experiment with new teaching methods, even methods that are difficult to implement and involve risks, because they expect their efforts will lead to positive results. They are able to internally minimize negative emotions and maintain belief that persistence will eventually produce desired results (Czerniak & Schriver-Waldon, 1991; Dutton, 1990; Hani, Czerniak, & Lumpe, 1996; Riggs & Enochs, 1990; Ross, 1992). Given that the phenomenon of efficacy strongly influences behavior, it is crucial for school administrators and project facilitators to be aware of, understand and nurture the efficacy levels of their teachers.

Recent research by Hoy and Hoy (2004) suggests that organizations, such as schools, can utilize and capitalize on efficacy to help teachers as a group achieve higher goals for student learning. Collective efficacy is a group construct that signifies a belief in the members that the group can achieve more than individuals can do alone.

Bandura (1994) states "perceived collective efficacy is defined as a group's shared belief in its conjoint capabilities to organize and execute the courses of action required to produce given levels of attainments" (p, 477). Groups who build collective efficacy have diverse membership with a variety of knowledge, competencies and experience. This group optimism is further influenced by how members interact with each other.

Respectful communication must be steadfastly enculturated and dialogue that builds rather than undermines is essential. Collective efficacy can be further influenced by certain professional development strategies such as collaboration among teacher teams, co-planning units and lessons, looking at student work together and co-teaching.

Proposing a Minor Tweak of the Current View of Professionalism: The Call for "Holonomy"

As we have discussed, teachers have historically guarded their autonomy, insisting that they need to maintain instructional decision making in order to provide the most effective educational experience for their students. While we assert that a certain level of teacher autonomy is crucial, we also contend that in this era of standardization, the construct of teacher autonomy is incomplete and leads to inconsistencies in student learning experiences. We argue that what teachers should be demanding is more "holonomy" in their working environment.

Originating from Greek roots, "holons" means whole while "on" signifies part. Although holonomy has an extensive history in the mathematical arena, it was first used to explain human behavior in 1972, when Arthur Koestler used it to reference the part-whole interaction. Since its introduction, the term "holonomy" is commonly used in systems thinking describing the larger picture where each participant retains his or her autonomy, yet simultaneously acknowledging membership in the larger organization.

Autonomy signifies that one is making decisions founded on personal preference and belief while holonomy signifies that one's decisions reflect the larger culture and group goals (see table 1.2). Holonomy versus autonomy is not just a matter of semantics; it addresses tensions that emerge when members of the public and administrators envision rogue teachers responding to their own preferences for content coverage and recall individualistic and independent tendencies of the culture of teaching reminiscent of the 1980s!

In a holonomous school system, each teacher is an autonomous individual who makes instructional decisions based on her knowledge of national, state, and local standards, the culture of the school, and the demographics of her students.

While conscientious teachers have always worked this way, the concept of holonomy brings into focus the troubling constraints a scripted or controlled curriculum has on that teacher's ability to be autonomous. Scripted curricula, designed by those far outside the classroom, and unaware of the diverse students and school culture, interfere with holonomy. A local, home-grown cur-

Table 1.2. Autonomy versus Holonomy in Education

Autonomy in Education	Holonomy in Education
Teachers are encouraged to make individual decisions	Teachers are encouraged to collaborate to make group decisions
Concern with focus on Teacher Efficacy	A focus on Collective Efficacy
Professional Development primarily centering on learning to employ skills and techniques	Professional Development primarily centering on group learning and professional knowledge
Leads to excellent learning experiences for some students in some years	Leads to continuous learning for students across their educational career

riculum reconciles that challenge and transcends the notion of an autonomous teacher functioning as part of a larger educational environment.

Intended Consequences

Our unintended consequence of boosting professional practice and knowledge of the entirety of literacy teachers as a collective can and should be one of the intended consequences that any district duplicating these efforts aims for.

In their new publication, *Professional Capital: Transforming Teaching in Every School,* Hargreaves and Fullan (2012) investigate the differences between how American education is viewed and supported versus other high-achieving nations' education. These authors state that our "competitors know that the main point is not the effect of the individual teacher, for better or for worse, here and there, that counts, but rather how you maximize the cumulative effect of many, many teachers over time for each and every student" (2012, p. 15–16). They go on to say, "Students do very well because they have a *series* of very good teachers—not by chance, but by design" (italics in original, p. 16).

What Hargreaves and Fullan are advocating—the transformation of the teaching staff *as a whole*—is the key to student achievement and one of the most positive outcomes of a curriculum reform endeavor like this one.

Spreading the Word: Growing New Buds

As this pilot group of teachers strengthens their own teaching practices, professional skill, and collective efficacy, awareness will naturally spread to fellow teachers not part of the pilot team. The message must always be positive. Even though the pilot teachers have been selected for their passion and optimism, a reminder to retain a positive attitude regarding the endeavor is recommended.

Informal networks of teachers are already in place and will serve as a positive reinforcement to pilot teachers if they sense the enthusiasm and commitment to a teacher-designed program. No one wants to be on a losing team. The pilot teachers must exude excitement and positive energy about what they are accomplishing. This energy has the likelihood of becoming a powerful growth potential for the entire school collective if given its due attention.

Naysayers

As the power of the collective is crucial, project managers need to be alert to any prolonged negative discussions of whether or not this endeavor can be achieved. These few naysayers may be unwilling to invest the amount of energy and work into the program for fear that the work they put in will be for naught, the school board won't approve of the program or the principal will reject it.

These are real concerns and may lead to sabotage of future innovations if they are not addressed. It is the responsibility of the Project Manager to keep all governing parties abreast of the amount of effort teachers are putting into this project and the magnitude of the difference it will make for students.

SUMMARY

The foundation for literacy reform begins with a core of committed, passionate, and knowledgeable teachers; the impetus could also be implanted by an equally passionate administrator. Strong, efficacious teachers need the opportunity to engage in a critical review of which literacy practices are already successful in the school/district as well as the opportunity to be fueled with the vision of what literacy instruction *could* be.

In order to nurture the collective efficacy of this pilot group, members should begin visiting each other's classroom and the classrooms of similarly minded teachers across their locale and exploring current research and literature regarding literacy instruction. Extended study will reinforce that they are already doing many great things in their classrooms and that, together, they have the capacity to make an even bigger difference for their students.

Chapter Two

The Design Stage

SNAPSHOT #2

On a cold Monday in January, the members of the Reading Review Team filled the school boardroom. Four of the district's reading specialists, along with the curriculum coordinator, made their pitch to the school board and superintendent. Respectfully, they asked for permission from the school board to create their own reading program.

The presentation was flawless. It was undeniable that this group of educators was determined to create a program that met the needs of the district's extremely diverse population while staying true to the standards. The proposal spoke of balancing autonomy with accountability while it highlighted the possibility to provide consistent reading instruction across the district at all levels and for all students regardless of which school they attended.

The school board voted unanimously in favor of the program and the boardroom boomed. The team had until December to create a "home-grown" program and to report back to the board with samples of the program and initial data. Later, over celebratory drinks, they tried to revel in the victory but in the back of the team members' minds two words prevailed, "Oh sh_t!"

Once the go-ahead was given by the governing bodies and pilot teachers' buy-in was established, it became necessary for the team to come to agreement on the conceptual model of the program. Agreement on philosophies of instruction, how time with students would be organized, and how standards would be dealt with allowed the teams to begin work in earnest.

A FRAMEWORK ON WHICH TO BUILD THE PROGRAM

In order for a home-grown program to be comprehensive and consistent from kindergarten to eighth grade, its creators must develop a framework and generate a set of necessary components central to each grade level. When beginning the curriculum creation process, it is helpful for the teacher-authors to come to agreement on:

- A curriculum calendar for each grade level's units
- An agreed-upon framework for how time is allocated during the literacy block
- A universal focus lesson structure
- One reading assessment to be used across the district, K–8
- A list of materials and resources necessary for each classroom teacher
- A universal screening tool

Tasks that will help maintain rigor and alignment to the state or national standards are:

- Unpack and truly understand the standards at each grade level
- Vertical alignment between all grade levels

Before any substantial work can be tackled, it is helpful for the project manager to remember that collegial conversation can quickly turn into inefficient discourse if a clear-cut plan is not in place. Roles must be designated and boundaries set, if progress is to be made. Determining and analyzing the standards for each grade level should be one of the first tasks of the group in order to keep their focus on track, and a comprehensive examination must be planned for, to take place within and between all grade levels. Vertical and horizontal alignment is crucial for rigorous instruction to take place with no room for ambiguity.

If the design team does not know what to teach, they will be at a loss for how to teach it. Back in 1999, just as the standards movement was gaining momentum, Schmidt and associates posited that some states' curricula could be considered "a mile wide and an inch deep." When the breadth of a standard is so vast, it can unintentionally get lost in translation, rendering the analysis useless.

One crucial component to a home-grown, standards-based program is that the writers must truly understand the expectations of the standards. This can be done by "unpacking" the standards. Although this phase of the project *could* be accomplished by individuals, such as administrators or teacher leaders, and given that the language of the standards tends to be ambiguous, it is highly recommended that professional discourse within teacher teams be the vehicle for unpacking the standards.

Grade-level teams spend time discussing and interpreting the very words of the standards, later rewriting them in kid-friendly terms. Finally, the standards are rewritten as outcome objectives for the children to understand and to assist with clarity; as the lessons are delivered, teachers explain and often post the outcome objectives in the classroom for the children to refer to in their day-to-day learning. Once the unpacking process is accomplished, the possibility of laying out the year in terms of a curriculum calendar is possible.

Having deep understanding and clarity of the content and rigor of the objectives affords the teachers with a vision of how to reach them. Creating the curriculum calendar opens up the possibility of finding ways to integrate content areas with literacy topics. The creation of a curriculum calendar does not imply that all teachers must teach the same lessons or units at the same time. It merely gives them a roadmap to follow without being militant.

Many core programs provide the teacher with a script. The script determines how long a teacher-directed lesson should be, how long a reading group should last, and it may even go so far as to connect the reading curriculum to thematic units which may or may not be relevant for the students.

While it may be suggested that a core program offers a multitude of choices for the teacher, it is impossible for a published program to be able to claim that it can meet the needs and interests of all students. When creating a child-centered program, the needs of the individual children, the climate of the classroom, and the culture of the school come first.

Since teachers take charge of the format in a home-grown program, it makes sense to create a lesson template that retains the professional autonomy of each teacher, while providing continuity between the schools, in a sense encouraging the curriculum to be holonomous. Although teachers can negotiate "how" instruction is delivered, they are responsible for teaching a specific set of standards.

By developing a holonomous structure of delivery, teachers stay on track, ensuring each student's instruction in reading is equitable to their peers' across the city, since all teachers at that grade level are using the same language. By no means does this insinuate a scripted curriculum; it simply provides all teachers and students with the materials necessary to level the playing field. By using common language, it fosters collegial conversation among all teachers across the district, enhancing a constant evolution of the program.

Research says that children should read independently for upwards of thirty to sixty minutes in the elementary grades, but how can this fit into an already overcrowded schedule? With a core program, this can pose a challenge.

It is eye opening, when we know that time spent practicing actual reading is the major factor in students' success in reading, yet when researchers investigate the amount of time students in classrooms that use a basal REALLY spend on reading, the results are staggering. The excerpts in many reading anthologies require no more than twenty to thirty minutes to read. If the excerpt is the main reading selection that students will be exposed to in a week-long instructional plan, students will have limited opportunities to practice their reading.

One major issue with basals or core curricula is that they tend to take up a great deal of instructional time on activities other than reading. There are phonics lessons, vocabulary lessons, some comprehension discussions, and lots and lots of worksheets. This "busy work" makes some teachers and administrators think they are giving their students a balanced academic workout; however, due to the extensive time these tasks take, they are actually hindering students' ability to practice reading.

When a program affords the flexibility necessary for children to experiment and implement newly learned reading strategies using books they have selected for themselves according to interest and level, they become more mindful and independent readers.

A convergence of research suggests that both emergent and established readers need time to process newly acquired skills—the more time children engage in meaningful reading and writing, the more proficient they become (Brause, Lee, & Moliterno 2008). For some students, a mere ten minutes of productive reading is all they can sustain during independent practice, but for their classmate, sixty minutes is reasonable.

A child-centered program's schedule adapts to the children's needs, providing time for both practice and enrichment. It provides ample time to read for those who are able to stay engaged and it provides options for the student who is more reluctant to sit alone for a lengthy period of time. With this flexibility, the teacher and student negotiate the curriculum together based on what the teacher knows about her children as readers and writers. She is able to adapt the readers' and writers' workshop to the climate of the class.

When researching the teaching practices of exemplary teachers in six states across the nation, Richard Allington found six common features demonstrated in the classrooms he observed.

- Time—a higher percentage of the day was spent with students actually engaged in reading. Students in these successful classrooms took part in more guided reading, independent reading, and content area reading. Focus lessons outlining a new skill were brief, some lasting as little as five minutes.
- Text—students are surrounded by differentiated levels of texts that are appropriate to all readers in the room. They practice decoding, fluency, and comprehension skills in texts that would be considered easy for them.

- Teach—scripted prepackaged programs only provide the teacher with a "definitional" model where the lesson focuses on simply explaining the skill at a generic level. Effective instruction requires teachers to teach strategies explicitly, but more importantly, it entails guidance in how to transfer the newly learned skill into the child's own independent practice at her or his level.
- Talk—effective literacy instruction includes more conversation and less interrogation for ALL students, regardless of reading level. Conversations with students about reading require the teacher to personalize and focus, relying on the responses of the students themselves rather than on a script.
- Tasks—students are given "managed choices." Differentiation is key when assigning and evaluating student work.
- Test—fewer test preparation activities are necessary because the instruction itself prepared students for what they would experience on the test (Allington 2002).

None of the six features that Allington and his observers noted can occur without knowing each child as a learner. It is obvious in this study that imperative to targeting all students' needs in a classroom are carefully thought-out and written lessons, dynamic resources available to students and teachers, and a schedule that affords the teacher the time necessary to cater all of her instruction to all of her students. In addition, this holistic approach to literacy instruction cannot happen without the administration supporting teachers and trusting that teachers, as autonomous decision makers, have the expertise necessary to match their instruction to their students.

In Braugner and Lewis's (2008) designation of the "thirteen core understandings about reading and learning to read," with respect to teachers' instructional choices, they contend that "teachers must consider the factors that support children's *learning* about print that are appropriate to children's *current* understanding." A child's instructional program that is designed, executed, and modified by her teacher can more appropriately support the acquisition of new skills if the teacher is able to make provisions based on each child's prior experiences. This philosophy is the antithesis of a pre-packaged core program.

A NEW LEADING ROLE

The reformation of reading instruction district-wide requires the involvement of all educators to some extent. Teacher empowerment and holonomy are the hallmarks of a teacher-created program; however, it is important to appoint one person to facilitate the components of the program. A point person is needed for collecting and analyzing data, keeping track of materials, and being mindful of the literacy schedule as well as serving as a knowledgeable and experienced resource for teachers.

But who can take on this role? These responsibilities are too extensive and specialized for a district to expect them to be effectively accomplished by a principal. A school that has a dedicated literacy coach already has a built-in resource for taking on these responsibilities. In districts where a literacy coach is not a current position, schools are encouraged to convert the duties of a reading specialist to that of literacy facilitator (as this position will be referred to throughout the rest of this book) to support this endeavor. We will discuss this process at length in chapter 4 and outline the position's responsibilities and duties.

We can hear what readers may be thinking, "What? Get rid of our reading specialist? Who will support the struggling readers?!" Our response will not be to tell you that it's because the teacher-created curriculum will be so foolproof that students will not need reading support anymore (that wouldn't be realistic).

We are going to suggest that since creating a teacher-designed program is an intense and time-consuming endeavor, it is imperative to support that effort with a knowledgeable individual who can keep track of and move the teachers through the curriculum. We can also say that, because of the embedded professional development that teachers have regular access to throughout the school year, the level of good, core instruction for all students will be raised through all classroom teachers becoming expert reading and writing teachers.

The position of the literacy facilitator is essential in maintaining continuity throughout the district. It is necessary for the literacy facilitators to remain in close contact. Constant consultation ensures cohesiveness within and between all schools. The literacy facilitators report regularly on what they see in the classrooms, and through weekly collaboration they address disparities immediately, as they happen.

For example, a literacy facilitator may notice that guided reading means different things to different people. Classroom libraries are resplendent in some rooms while downright empty in others. The way the libraries are set up can be yet another issue that needs addressing. Focus lessons that are intended to last ten to fifteen minutes may drone on sometimes for upwards of a half hour. Word study is taught on an individual basis in some classes, while in others generic spelling lists are given.

Teacher autonomy is integral but continuity and consistency between the classrooms and schools is of equal importance and should be addressed with urgency (e.g., holonomy). If the program is to work as its creators intended, the facilitator is the lifeline that connects all teachers.

Housed at each elementary school, living and breathing the program with the teacher, the facilitator has her finger on the pulse of the program each day. She is in the "trenches" with the teachers and knows the individual and overarching limitations. We have found in our work that when a need arises in one building, it signifies an undiagnosed, identical need in another building. This makes it easy to provide professional development in a timely fashion.

Although teachers must be respected and entrusted to control their personal learning, the literacy facilitator provides guidance, pedagogical instruction and practical grounding for teachers, administrators, and students.

Literacy facilitators continually compile a list of needs and make ongoing workshops and job-embedded PD opportunities available to the teachers. In a perfect world, time would be given to all teachers to visit one another at their own building and across the city, but in this profession, that time and the resources necessary for such an endeavor are limited. Invaluable professional development opportunities exist in just about all classrooms.

In our experience, once the literacy facilitators spent time in various classrooms, they realized that teacher leaders were among their colleagues; their exemplary practices needed to be showcased in order to better literacy instruction on a more global level. One approach was through video. The high school technology class was approached with the request to film, edit, and produce a video outlining the common components of the teacher-created literacy curriculum. Students were thrilled with this opportunity and the design team was equally thrilled with the final result!

Through this video, the district was able to set the groundwork for the professional development. For a new teacher to the building or a teacher needing reinforcement, the video is a useful tool that outlines and illustrates all of the expectations, from how to teach to a focus lesson to the format for guided reading groups. When teachers watch the video, they are better able to realize their own strengths and areas of need with respect to professional development.

In a way, this video has become a sort of public relations tool for the district's teacher-created program. It is a glimpse into what happens during reading/writing instruction across the city in kindergarten through eighth grade.

PROFESSIONAL DEVELOPMENT:
A NECESSARY INGREDIENT IN READING REFORM

It is common to find districts embedding teacher-workshop days or early-release days into their school calendars. Although the intention is good, sometimes teachers feel time could be better spent focusing on their own professional development rather than on what the district has "directed" them to do. Sometimes teachers know and can articulate what they are lacking pedagogically and in what areas they need to grow, but others need guidance to make that determination.

Often, if given the time to be reflective, a teacher will target her areas of lesser strength but districts fall flat in their ability to provide their teachers with the time and resources necessary to address those areas.

For literacy instruction to be reformed system-wide, all teachers in the district need to see themselves as researchers—that is, introspective practitioners who continuously look for ways to grow alongside their students. Without inquiry, instruction is weak, making way for autonomy and holonomy to be replaced with directives. Simply put, they must stay atop methods that have been proven to work. Allington (2002) asserts that a series of studies concludes that "good teachers, effective teachers, matter much more than particular curriculum materials, pedagogical approaches, or 'proven programs.'"

Administrators who realize the need for classroom teachers to possess the same knowledge as a reading specialist understand the need for professional development that targets all aspects of literacy instruction. Classroom teachers, particularly in the primary grades, must be given tools so that they can provide comprehensive, inclusive, and differentiated instruction based on the changing needs of the students. For example, a first-grade teacher may not be able teach a student how to comprehend better if she does not address decoding issues that are impacting that child's fluency.

FULL INCLUSION

The need for professional development that targets all aspects of literacy instruction also holds true for the administrators themselves. When administrators, regardless of prior experience and background, see themselves as instructional leaders in literacy, they begin to make time for and value the professional opportunities given in their district. Realizing what they do *not* know is half the battle. Inviting them to develop professionally alongside their teachers is the next step if they are expected to be a partner in reforming reading instruction.

Simultaneously, opportunities to continue learning about literacy development also provide them with tools they need to better evaluate teachers in their literacy instruction. They know the correct questions to ask; they know when they see exemplary teaching and they are willing to support their teachers as researchers. Kucer (2008) argues that teachers know how to ask the right questions based on the needs of their students. They want to read about topics, experiment with methods, and explore resources in order to learn how to support their students' growth.

If this is expected of teachers, perhaps the same should be expected of administrators. In chapter 5, we will further discuss the necessity of professional development relating to the idea of teacher "renewal" as it correlates directly to reforming literacy instruction. We will further explore and illustrate how job-embedded professional development is delivered as part of a teacher-created reading program and supported by the administration.

The necessity of including administrators on the bottom floor of any reform can be illustrated through an example of problems that occurred when our district reformed literacy instruction. The struggles we faced could have derailed the progress of the teacher-created program, yet they could have been averted relatively easily.

As the teachers, reading specialists, and curriculum coordinator enthusiastically dove into the tasks of creating lessons after unpacking the standards and agreeing to the child-centered frameworks of our program, principals knew little of the program's objectives; this neglect engendered skepticism among the school leaders.

When pieces of the program were implemented in classrooms across the district, principals became downright uneasy. They imagined their test scores plummeting as they envisioned classrooms in a wild-west scenario where anything would go depending on the whim of the teachers. Combine a limited knowledge of literacy instruction with the teachers' new sense of empowerment and it's enough to make a principal downright horrified. Principals anticipated teachers teaching whatever they wanted and when they wanted, while the disciplined rigor they believed existed in their classrooms was thrown out the window.

It appeared as though they were losing power as a revolution began taking shape within their schools. Interestingly enough, few on the design team were aware of principals' anxiety, but once their fear was recognized, they were included in discussions and decision making, even if they were unable to attend the meetings.

As the program creation moved forward, the literacy facilitators helped principals develop a general understanding of the research base in literacy by actively walking principals through classrooms where they could witness teachers implementing components of the program. The principals were astonished. Wanting to know more, they became supportive partners in the process and began to see their teachers as literacy leaders who knew their craft and sought ways to constantly improve themselves.

Booth and Rowsell (2002) stress the need for all principals to be "literacy principals" who possess an interest in and even a passion for literacy, in addition to working knowledge about literacy and language development. They work with their staff to plan, launch, and monitor literacy initiatives, or support others in this endeavor. In an age where the demands of a principal are far beyond budgets and teacher evaluation, administrators have little choice but to share their leadership. Slowly, they came to terms with the magnitude of the change and warmed up to the notion that they, too, were learners in this process.

ASSESSMENTS AND ACCOUNTABILITY

Assessment is imperative when determining the success of students, teachers, and the program. Without such benchmarks, there is no way to know if the program's content meets the standards and addresses the needs of the students, or if the level of rigor is on track. Just as fidelity is a critical element to the reliability of a program, it is equally important when observing a child's reading behavior.

Teachers as assessors require ongoing professional development in order to administer reading assessments with validity. Utilizing running records or diagnostic reading inventories affords the teacher the data necessary when determining a student's reading level. From these assessments, she is able to view her students through a formative and summative lens. A miscue analysis taken from a reading inventory shows the teacher such things as whether or not the student needs work on decoding strategies or recognizing sight words and how these behaviors impact comprehension and fluency.

Although an informal reading inventory is quick and can be done multiple times throughout the year, if professional development is not accessible for teachers administering these assessments, the validity of the data generated is subpar. The delivery methods can vary among those administering the assessment, while the analysis and final scoring of the test can pose a variety of idiosyncrasies.

Again, teachers must work toward calibrating their interpretations of data. This is best accomplished through constant conversation, modeling, observation, and analysis of data throughout the school year. All personnel administering reading assessments are more apt to stay on the same page if they are constantly "reminded" of proper procedure. These ongoing diagnostic assessments inform the teacher's knowledge of how her students are progressing and inform her instructional decisions, but are they enough?

A Necessary Evil

While informal assessments are crucial for tracking individual student progress and informing a teacher's instruction, they remain informal and their subjectivity can misinform targeted instruction. Teachers may rely on their own knowledge of literacy development to make instructional decisions rather than on valid data. No amount of shared conversation and professional development will erase the human side of informal assessments.

Teachers will naturally critique student work based on their own criteria and understanding, but a reliable safety net is a necessary component if the stakeholders are to be assured that students are learning the requisite standards.

A core literacy program is backed by a large educational publishing house that has the resources to pay for powerful education researchers to write components of their programs and to undertake scientific studies on their material, whereas a teacher-written curriculum does not have that luxury.

So, what is a school district to do? The school board, administration, and parents have the right to demand that the curriculum be rigorous and based on the current research. Waiting for the standardized information generated by a state or national test is not a time-sensitive option; and although teachers are comfortable with the results of their informal assessment and cringe at the thought of more testing, they are aware that an informal reading inventory may not provide the information necessary to target the root of the problem a child has while reading. One way to approach this quandary is to design practical, user-friendly and manageable *common formative assessments*.

Ideally, Common Formative Assessments (CFA) are short, four-to-six question tests that only require minutes to administer. They can be implemented as the school day begins, prior to a transition, or at the end of the day. It is crucial that these CFAs be designed to be scored in a timely manner by the teacher, thus rendering the information applicable immediately.

In order to meet the requirement of standardization, these CFAs must reflect the common core standards, rather than the objectives of the program. This, in turn, ensures the curriculum does, in fact, match the standards and prepare students for a state or national assessment. The CFAs become the unifying component between the innovative curriculum, the diverse professional knowledge of the teachers, and the standards.

Although the use of common formative assessments requires a slight change in routine, teachers report that the information they generate is valuable and the cost-to-benefit ratio is worth their efforts. A section in chapter 3 will be devoted to outlining the process of creating formative assessments.

A TIME TO REFLECT

Change requires feedback. We cannot institute change then run away from it, merely hoping that it was the right decision or that it will last. In a home-grown reading program, the heart of its anatomy is its teachers. If the voices of those teachers are not listened to, failure is immanent. Teachers need time to celebrate successes and brainstorm ways to address issues that arise within the school year.

One optimal time for collaboration is at the conclusion of the school year when the events of the prior year are still fresh in people's minds. Professional development cannot end once the 180 days are over, nor can we expect teachers to forego summer vacation plans for PD opportunities.

By "inviting" teachers to come together immediately after the last day of school to debrief and discuss their literacy successes and disappointments, the program is strengthened along with the teachers' sense of value. When teachers are told that their opinion, ideas, or suggestions are vital for the program to evolve, they feel empowered. This empowerment continues the teacher's investment in the program. It is a win-win situation but requires the time and money of the district.

It is surprising how much impact one or two days at the conclusion of the school year can have on tired teachers as they begin their summer vacation. Somehow they manage to find the energy to begin thinking about how to better their instruction in the year to come using the lessons they learned from the previous year.

Undoubtedly, they will use the summer weeks to reinvent instruction that did not go as planned or read professional materials others found useful over the prior year. Administrators can also plan accordingly, based on the articulated needs of their teachers. They may create future schedules differently or better plan early-release days. The synchronicity between the two camps continues throughout the summer break.

Reforming reading instruction is based on "proaction," not reaction. Time for reflection is integral if we expect teachers to "reorganize and improve"— the ultimate definition of reform.

SUMMARY

An agreed-upon framework for the envisioned program is critical to set the foundation as a powerful reinforcing growth potential and to act as an anchor to each grade level's progress. This foundation includes the philosophy of the program, the organization of the program and the establishment of common materials used in the program. The framework includes grounding decisions to national and local standards and the assessment systems that will indicate student achievement. Full inclusion of students, teachers, and administrators is recommended to be nonnegotiable, and the creation of the position of facilitator of teacher efforts is recommended.

Once the framework is debated and discussed, teachers can begin their work collectively and individually, filling in the templates and communicating through technology.

Chapter Three

The Production Stage

Teachers on the design team gathered on their first day of summer vacation to begin writing the reading portion of their home-grown literacy program. They would return for two more days to continue their work, as well as devote time throughout the summer to continue the process. The dedication and ambition was infectious—at least for the first couple of hours.

Like excited school children on the first day of school, the teachers (soon to be writers) began to discuss the plan of attack that had been outlined by the curriculum coordinator. They were charged with unpacking the standards, creating grade-level curriculum calendars, devising a structure for the reading block, and creating a set of lessons for each standard. But, by noon of the first day, all hell broke loose.

Passions flared as egos were squelched, expectations diminished, and power plays took place all around the room. Teachers stormed out of the room, threatening not to return. It was downright ugly, but the rest of the group plodded on. Those who stayed and those who later composed themselves and returned, reminded themselves of the reasons they were there—the district's students. They were mindful of this opportunity that they had been granted, with the full trust of the administrators, school board, and parents.

History was being made. They were the founding mothers/fathers of a program that would forever change the way literacy was taught in the district. By the end of the three days, standards were unpacked, curricula aligned, lessons created, and the joy that was present in the room on the first morning finally returned.

This chapter is arranged into sections based on the components of one possible literacy framework. It utilizes a variety of best practices. The examples given are primarily for reading instruction; however, the framework for writing instruction is similar. It begins with the fundamentals—curriculum calendar, scope and sequence, and unpacked standards—and then moves into the actual structure of the 60/90 minute reading block, and illustrates the readers' workshop, focus lesson, guided/independent reading, and assessments.

We will also share the variety of ways in which teachers can maximize the literacy block in order to incorporate reading in the content areas, vocabulary, and word study. Everything is designed through teacher-led, collaborative efforts matching the academic needs of the students and philosophical beliefs of the faculty.

Each teacher or administrator reading this may interpret it a bit differently, but the bottom line is that whatever format is used, the instruction aligns with the standards, allows teachers to exercise their professional creativity, and provides all students with the tools necessary for success.

We cannot stress enough that the materials presented here are simply physical manifestations of the foundation of one conceptualized curriculum. While these documents serve to hold and display one way of thinking, the foundation of literacy reform remains the knowledge, skill, and professionalism of the teachers as a collective. Focused professional discussions and collaboration are the true outcomes and the driving force of reform.

We include this chapter as an example of a possible outcome of this type of reform, but insist that if these documents were simply handed to teachers as a curriculum without the professional conversation, the potential would be there for teachers to treat it as a script and for administrators to demand strict adherence to the script. That is not our intent.

CURRICULUM CALENDAR

A variety of factors must come into play as teachers decide *when* to teach *what*. Even though a home-grown program affords the teachers the flexibility to teach the curriculum by way of a natural progression that feels right to them, it is important in the design process to create a calendar of units that provides a timeline that *guides* teachers in order to ensure all standards are taught. It is crucial to keep in mind that the curriculum calendar stays as a guide with flexibility at its heart. It is by no means a mandated schedule.

A calendar is also extremely important in order to keep all who support literacy on the same page—interventionists, literacy facilitators, and administrators. Its role is multifaceted. For example, should a principal be interested in performing a series of literacy walk-throughs that focus on second-grade classrooms, prior to the walk-through the principal will be prepared for what she will observe. She will know what skills to look for and what types of conversations she might have with the students. If the school's literacy facilitator is planning professional development opportunities, her focus will become more relevant and time sensitive.

And finally, interventionists working with students outside of the classroom are aware of the skills and strategies students are responsible for practicing as they read. The paraprofessional, reading specialist, or special education teacher stays abreast of the current focus lessons, thus eliminating the incoherent, piecemeal instruction typically given to below-grade-level students who are pulled out of the class for extra support.

Regardless of the child's ability, she is able to practice strategies that fellow classmates are practicing in their guided reading groups or during independent practice. Classroom teachers and support staff even the playing field for all children when a cohesive curriculum is in place. The curriculum calendar is (see table 3.1), in a sense, a checks-and-balances tool for all involved in a child's instruction.

UNPACKING THE STANDARDS

Before lessons can be written and teachers can decide which resources to purchase, all members of the design team must familiarize themselves with the standards. By "unpacking" each grade level's standard, the teachers truly understand through careful scrutiny and analysis what their students are required to learn while in their classroom. The teachers determine if and when the standard appears on the state test; acknowledge the level at which it was expected to be learned using Bloom's Taxonomy and Webb's Depth of Knowledge; and finally, put the standard into kid-friendly terms called "I can" statements.

Although the above steps are extremely time-consuming and at times daunting tasks, the results are multifaceted. Through careful examination of the standards, teachers begin to intimately understand what their students are expected to know by the time they leave their classroom in June. They also familiarize themselves with the level of rigor with which the skill needs to be taught.

Rather than just being a list of standards, the grade-level expectations are spelled out in language that makes sense to everyone, including the students. From there, the design team can take what they know about their student

Table 3.1. Example of Second Grade Curriculum Calendar

	Curriculum Calendar Reading/Writing Workshop				
Months	Units (writing units are in bold)	Standards Addressed	Common Formative Assessment	Other Formative Assessments	Content Area Units
August/September	Launching Reading/ Writing Workshop	Common Core Standards go here		Benchmarks Writing prompt	Teachers tie Social Studies/ Science into literary curriculum
October	Decoding strategies **Conventions (ongoing)**		#1 Word identification	Reading/writing conferences Running records	
November	Story elements **Writing Narratives**		#2 Character and setting	Reading/writing conferences Running records	
December/January	Comprehension strategies **Responding to Literature**		#3 Using context clues	Benchmark as appropriate Reading/writing conferences	

population and create child-centered focus lessons. They can provide lists of materials that they need for their lessons, including mentor texts, graphic organizers, and professional development resources.

Many schools across the nation have already engaged in the task of unpacking state standards. Those systems already have a solid understanding of what students should know and be able to do to meet state standards. As the nation progresses toward the Common Core State Standards (CCSS), schools may find, as we did, that they need to readjust depth of knowledge and instructional rigor. A literacy reform initiative is an ideal time to meld expectations for student outcomes.

READERS' WORKSHOP STRUCTURE

The organization of the readers' workshop is open to a variety of possibilities; however, the amount of time allotted for it plays a crucial role in its structure and how the teacher utilizes the time. If the schedule allows for it, a ninety-minute, undisturbed time is ideal but a sixty-minute block will also work (see figure 3.1).

The first ten to fifteen minutes is used for the delivery of the daily focus lesson followed by a flexible guided-reading schedule. If teachers plan on rotating two to three guided-reading groups in the time that follows the focus lesson, there will be enough time at the end of the workshop for about five minutes to wrap up and share. Some teachers opt to use part of the readers'

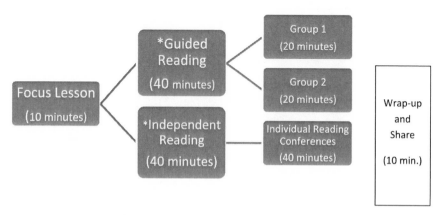

Figure 3.1.   Readers' Workshop Model.
*Teachers have the option of rotating through two guided reading groups once the focus lesson is complete or reading individually with students.

workshop to integrate literacy-based content-area materials, vocabulary, and word-study work.

The teachers of this program believe strongly that students should read for the duration of the readers' workshop, but they are realistic. They are mindful that students require copious amounts of time for sustained silent reading if they are going to develop into strategic readers. For those students who are not yet at that point, teachers provide options that are literacy-based and chosen by the individual student. It is always a teacher's objective to have all students reading just-right books for 100 percent of the readers' workshop time, but until that is possible, they find ways to "maximize the literacy block." We will discuss this model further in the chapter.

This structure for readers' workshop will work in most elementary school settings. Middle school teachers may need to modify the times, due to schedule requirements and/or other confinements. We found that at the middle school, the language arts blocks tend to be less than ninety-minutes or even less than sixty. In that short amount of time, teachers are expected to encompass reading, writing, word study, and vocabulary instruction. Although a seemingly insurmountable task, teachers can make it work by rotating and integrating their instruction in order to target all literacy skills in collaboration with the core subject teachers, such as social studies and science teachers.

Focus Lesson Format

The beginning of the literacy block typically begins with a ten to fifteen minute focus lesson (see table 3.2). Although the terminology may be different, a readers' or writers' workshop format is usually kicked off with direct instruction that focuses the children on a particular skill or topic. Since consistency and a common language are hallmarks of a teacher-created program, it is better to provide classroom teachers with a written lesson for each standard.

It is important to make clear that, although the lessons are explicit and may even appear to be "script-like" to some, they are presented to the teachers as *tools*. The depth with which teachers follow them is up to their own discretion. Some teachers might post the focus lesson at their teaching easel as they deliver instruction, while some simply use the lesson as a guide for their teaching. Regardless, each teacher remains mindful that all standards must be taught throughout the year. Remember, only the "what" is nonnegotiable. "How" the instruction is delivered is flexible and open to teacher creativity.

Teachers are inherently creative people. This is apparent in the elaborate lessons and units delivered on a daily basis in America's classrooms. Teachers are reluctant to forego or replace lessons that they created, but when teachers pool their creativity in order to write lessons for all to use, the results

Table 3.2. Example of Focus Lesson Template

Unit: Reading/Writing Focus:	Standard

Lesson	*Teacher Actions*
Explanation of Focus:	
Resources/Materials:	
Modeled instruction:	
Guided Practice:	
Independent Practice:	
Conclusion/share:	

can be remarkable. Within that process, a bit of consternation may occur. Although teachers may gain a cache of valuable lessons and units, they may also be asked to replace their old lessons with the new ones if their old lessons are not consistent with the program's language or aligned to the standards.

Efficiency is key when it comes to writing focus lessons. Some people are better at it than others. By devising a plan and targeting the team's exemplary writers, the work is less taxing and produces results more quickly. Equally important is that all teachers receive the professional development on how to write lessons and, eventually, may be asked to contribute a few of their own to their grade level's focus lesson bank.

Once all the focus lessons are complete, one person for each grade level becomes a part of the revision and editing team. Here, lessons are reviewed for accuracy, efficacy, and precision. Grammar, punctuation, and spelling are edited so that the final product is of a professional grade. The program's focus lessons are reviewed at the conclusion of each school year and revisions are made if necessary.

The district administrators who opt out of purchasing a prewritten, pre-packaged, core program most likely do so because they feel that the material does not speak to *their* students. They cannot find one program that targets the specific needs of the students sitting in *their* classrooms. In a teacher-designed program, every focus lesson is written with *their* children in mind. They know students' backgrounds, their home-life situations, their class sizes, and their teachers' teaching styles. They understand the district's expectations and the expectations parents have of them. The lessons are customized to their clients (see table 3.3).

Guided Reading

The guided reading portion of the readers' workshop is considered to be one of the most crucial instructional components of this particular home-grown program. Based on the research surrounding guided reading, this small group setting allows teachers to instruct children on various reading strategies in texts that are at an instructional level appropriate for them. The teacher incorporates the day's focus lesson into her small group instruction as well as targets the individual or group's needs as readers.

Since there is no anthology included in the program, it is an absolute necessity that teachers have access to a wide variety of books at varying levels. The instruction must be purposeful and delivered in a timely and efficient manner in order to maximize the teachers' and students' time. Especially in an age where classroom sizes are soaring, small-group instruction, by way of the guided reading model, is a mainstay in the readers' workshop.

Over the years and within our work in various classrooms, we realized that many teachers come from a variety of guided reading experiences. Some have had the great fortune to receive training, while others managed to learn by doing. Regardless of the depth of knowledge in this area, it is important that, through professional development, guided reading be taught with consistency, continuity, and confidence.

The following are guidelines teachers across a district may use as their program's backbone ensuring all students are receiving small-group instruction

Table 3.3. Example of Second Grade Focus Lesson

Unit: Nonfiction/Information Text Reading Focus: Content Vocabulary	Standard

Lesson	Teacher Actions
Explanation of Focus:	*When we read nonfiction texts, we encounter a variety of new words that are linked to the subject we are reading about. As we begin learning more about the topic, we are better able to understand the meaning of these words and the differences between them.* *Ex: If I were reading a book about marine life, by the end of the book, I would be able to explain the differences between a mammal, fish, and a mollusk.*
Resouces/Materials:	*Any nonfiction text—particularly one that has content vocabulary in bold.
Modeled Instruction:	*When reading nonfiction texts, it is important to pay attention to the new words that are being introduced. Let me show you a few words that you may see in this book we're about to read. Right now, these words are probably unfamiliar to you but after we read the book together, you will have a better understanding of what these words mean.* Read text to students asking students to give a thumbs-up when they hear one of those words. Stop at various points where new content vocabulary is introduced to discuss meaning.
Guided Practice:	*Now that we finished the book and you have a better understanding of what these words mean, you can define them and compare them. Let's talk about how these words connect to the text.*
Independent Practice:	*As you read your nonfiction book, pay close attention to the words that are specific to the topic and write them down on your Post-it note. We will have an opportunity to share your new vocabulary with each other.*
Conclusion/Share:	Students may volunteer to share their words and connect them to the topic.

that is catered to their individual needs while the model remains consistent within and between all schools.

- Groups should be formed based on students' instructional level.
- No more than 4–5 per group.
- A minimum of twenty minutes, three times a week for students on or above grade level.
- Students below grade level need five days a week of guided reading with a trained teacher/paraprofessional.
- The day's focus lesson is addressed and reinforced during the guided strategy/reading group time.

Individual Reading Conference

Talking with readers one-on-one about their personal development helps maintain student motivation as well as strengthen the connection between teacher knowledge of students and the various interests and ability levels in the classroom. Individual reading conferences give the teacher access to align knowledge of standards *and* knowledge of students to the most appropriate curriculum materials and instructional strategies for each learner.

A number of teachers feel that they can individualize instruction more effectively by way of individual reading conferences rather than through guided reading groups. Although more time-consuming, these teachers believe that in order to know each child in their classroom as a reader, they must sit with each student and together engage in meaningful conversation about a text. They also feel that as they read with students one on one, they are consistently engaged in deep authentic reading assessment.

In an age when class sizes are growing and the burden of content exposure is increasing, meeting with all students individually becomes a luxury few can afford to maintain in their classrooms. In this program, the flexibility is always there for those teachers who are able to forego the guided reading model and meet regularly with their students on an individual basis. They key word here is *regularly*.

A teacher who can dedicate a set amount of time to each student on an individual basis for regular reading conferences should take full advantage of it. But should the time management become an issue that precludes students from individualized instruction, it is time for the teacher to re-evaluate how he sets up his readers' workshop time. It is better for a student to meet with a teacher in a small group multiple times in a week than for a student to not meet at all with her teacher.

Many teachers find that a balance of two models works in their classrooms. Readers who are above grade level tend to meet in small groups two to three times per week and individually with their teacher once or twice a week. Since readers who are at- or below-grade level are seen in small groups three to five times a week, and one component of the guided reading lesson is to read with each student individually, the majority of their reading conference is embedded within their small group time.

Teachers find creative ways to know their students as readers but the accountability piece is crucial here. Anecdotal record keeping is important for the teacher, principal, parents, and literacy facilitator. It should be clear to anyone who sets foot in classrooms across the district that all teachers know every one of their students, holistically, as readers.

Independent Reading

Interestingly, the component of the readers' workshop that is considered to be the most valuable by teachers and reading researchers alike was met with the most resistance from administrators. Administrators saw students reading books and teachers chatting with students but they did not see the direct, explicit instruction they were expecting. What they failed to realize is that after the direct instruction of the focus lesson, students need time to practice that skill.

For too long, we have saturated students with information and then allotted them no time to practice. Independent reading is crucial for interpreting and reconstructing newly acquired ideas into one's own thoughts and cementing those thoughts into long-term memories. Accountable independent reading is the backbone of a readers' workshop.

In this particular model that we have highlighted, every student reads every day on his or her own for a period of time. Because this is a monitored time, it requires a large amount of legwork on the part of the teacher. He must ensure that all students are matched to appropriate texts, that they are focused and utilizing the strategies that they were taught, and that they are enjoying the process.

Struggling readers, in particular, are guided toward texts that are comfortable for them and are checked on more frequently by the classroom teacher or support staff working in the room. All students are responsible for keeping track of their reading either in their readers' notebook or in a reading log. They implement the strategy that was the focus of the day's lesson and are prepared to share any discoveries during the end of the readers' workshop.

The teachers who designed this program fought for independent reading to be a mainstay in their daily reading instruction based on the research that shows students who read more are the ones who read better and attain higher reading achievement (Routman, 2003). These teachers worked tirelessly to dispel the notion that independent reading time equals free choice time. They held firmly to the belief that if we want to get better at something, the only way is through regular, sometimes arduous practice.

COMMON FORMATIVE ASSESSMENTS AND THEIR CALENDAR

It is easy to make excuses and blame failure on others. Few people enjoy accountability but it is a reality that all educators are facing in today's educational climate. However, finding the most appropriate accountability measure eludes many decision makers in education.

En masse, summative assessments may be efficient to administer but provide a mere snapshot of who our students are as learners. Oftentimes the information we receive from them is too broad and the results untimely, providing little useful information regarding a teacher's efficacy. Although educators cannot avoid the mandates that the governing bodies place with respect to evaluating our teachers and students, we can focus our attention on our students' learning at the grassroots level and in a way that is effective and constructive through teacher-created, relevant assessments.

Benjamin Franklin once said, "He that is good for making excuses is seldom good for anything else." There is no room for excuses when it comes to reading instruction. With one guiding objective, teachers who set out to create their own reading program can reform the way reading instruction is delivered in their district as they create lifelong, ardent readers.

This does not imply, however, that just because a child is a strong reader she is a passionate one. This passion many feel for the written word is subjective—teachers and administrators cannot expect 100 percent of their students to *love* reading. They can, however, commit themselves to teaching reading with a sense of fervor, so that all students leave school with an understanding and appreciation for the written word.

Accountability in a teacher-designed program is necessary for two reasons. First, there must be some way of assessing the efficacy of the program. Second, all teachers must take on the responsibility of teaching the standards in a way that is responsive to the needs of their students.

One option is the *common formative assessment* (see table 3.4). Teachers create a series of five to seven question probes connected to a set of essential standards for their grade level. The quick assessments are given throughout the year and are embedded in each unit, meaning shortly after the standard is taught, the students are assessed. They are administered based on a teacher-created common formative assessment calendar.

For example, a series of lessons on vocabulary knowledge will be taught over a period of days or perhaps a week. Once those lessons are complete,

Table 3.4. Example of a Second Grade Common Formative Assessment for Synonyms and Antonyms:

Name_____   Date_____

CC.2.L.5 Shows breadth of vocabulary knowledge, demonstrating understanding of word meanings or relationships by identifying synonyms or antonyms; or categorizing words. Read each sentence. Circle the word that means the same as the underlined word.

1. A growling dog is enought to *frighten* anyone.
   A. trip
   B. hurt
   C. scare
   D. trick

2. While Marcus looked for treasure he *discovered* a cave.
   A. dug
   B. found
   C. entered
   D. left

3. Kaya raised here hand in class but gave one wrong answer. She made an *error* in her thinking.
   A. sign
   B. job
   C. mark
   D. error

Read each sentence. Circle the word that means the opposite of the underlined word.

4. The mailman rang the door bell at the *front* door but only one dog heard him.
   A. back
   B. first
   C. side
   D. new

5. Tate wants to *sell* two cars today.
   A. fix
   B. buy
   C. make
   D. find

6. Zoe got in trouble because her desk was *filthy*.
   A. cold
   B. noisy
   C. dusty
   D. clean

the teacher administers the common formative assessment that evaluates students' level of understanding of that particular skill, perhaps synonyms and antonyms. All teachers in a grade level would administer that assessment during the same week.

Some flexibility is given with respect to the precise day but for the most part, assessments are usually given at the end of the week. Since teachers at each grade level are following the same curriculum calendar, timing is not an issue. Based on the results of the assessment, the teacher gains an understanding of his instructional efficacy. The information lets the teacher know immediately which student understands the skill, needs reinforcement, or perhaps could benefit from enrichment. Teachers decide at their grade level how they will target those students.

Typically, teachers reinforce or enrich the skills in the classroom during guided reading or independent reading conferences. Often, a correlation between the students' reading level and the outcomes of their assessments is apparent, so the guided reading time works well for reinforcing the skills. For those cases where the two are not so synchronized, the teacher may ask for the support of the reading specialist or paraprofessional to ensure the skills are addressed.

A teacher may also use the independent reading conference as a time to address areas of misunderstanding and, since the grade level is assessing the skill at the same time, flexibly grouping between classrooms is also an option. After about a week, students are reassessed. Teachers record the progress of each student and are mindful of anyone who may need further practice.

It is also important to vertically align all of the essential standards among the grade levels in order to find out where overlaps and gaps occurred. This time-consuming yet valuable task affords each grade level the opportunity to see which standard was over-taught and which standard was overlooked or not taught to the degree it should. For example, predicting is taught in just about every elementary grade. Although predicting is a necessary skill that all readers must be taught, it does not need to be focused on at every grade level throughout a child's elementary school career.

Through the time spent vertically aligning the essentials standards, the teachers may agree to introduce predicting as a skill and assess it in first grade and during the subsequent years only review and reinforce it. Because of this, other reading strategies such as inferring and synthesizing can receive more emphasis in the intermediate grades. There is potential for this to happen with a variety of essential standards; therefore, the vertical alignment process is a key step in the creation of a school or district-wide program.

SCOPE AND SEQUENCE

Just about any prepackaged, core program on the market today comes with a scope and sequence somewhere in the teacher's manual. It is predictability that sells the program to both teachers and administrators. An explicitly laid out list of skills and strategies expected to be taught at any given grade level takes the guesswork away from teachers teaching the program. Autonomous teaching is a wonderful thing as long as the material being taught is relevant, appropriately comprehensive, and sequential. Vertically aligning the curriculum is discussed in more detail in chapter 5.

In addition to the vertical alignment, the teachers who created the teacher-designed program felt strongly that a scope and sequence needed to be developed and included in the program in order to provide yet another safety net. Found at the front of every grade level's program binder, the scope and sequence lays out their "nonnegotiables" for the school year in an extremely user-friendly format. Teachers are invited to write on them and check in with their grade-level teammates in order to track their progress throughout the year.

The scope and sequence is a guide for the teachers and literacy facilitators; it is not an evaluative tool for the principal. It was never intended for that purpose and will never be used in that manner. It has, however, provided some insight for the principals as to what information students are expected to know by the end of each grade level and, for many teachers, is used simply as a checklist to ensure they have covered the standards specific to their grade level.

FLEXIBLE GROUPING/MAXIMIZING THE LITERACY BLOCK: OPTIONS FOR THE READERS' WORKSHOP

Since the literacy block is intended to last a minimum of sixty minutes of a child's school day, it was critical to learn just what students were doing during that time. As the literacy facilitators, principals, and curriculum coordinators began to visit classrooms to observe program implementation, it became apparent that silent reading did not mean the same for all students.

Undoubtedly, there are children at every grade level who can sustain silent reading for as long as their teacher allows them. They are engaged and stimulated and need little guidance in their reading development. Conversely, there are students whose attention span or skill level is such that to expect them to engage in a text for more than a few minutes is simply unreasonable. These students tend to find much more "creative" ways to spend their time.

In a perfect world, all students would sit quietly and comfortably reading a "just-right" book of their choice for thirty to forty-five minutes while their teacher conducts guided reading groups or individual reading conferences with their peers. But an experienced teacher knows that this may not always happen for all students all of the time. There are those students who could be up for the next academy award in "acting" like a reader, while others have mastered the art of monopolizing the teacher's time by requiring copious amounts of "redirection." To address discrepancies in student reading stamina, teachers develop options in order to maximize the literacy block, while still promoting and expecting reading at all times.

Most students are seen at least three times a week in a guided reading group which uses about twenty minutes of their literacy block, leaving them with approximately thirty minutes of independent reading time. On days when they are not seen, they could be faced with upwards of forty-five minutes of reading on their own. In order to maximize this time, some teachers integrate other subject matter through literacy-based activities (see table 3.5).

Students are given a menu at the onset of each week that is expected to be completed after a set period. As the student completes the activities, she checks off what is completed. At the top of the list is silent reading, and the time requirement is specified.

Literacy-based activities may include students writing in their reader's notebook, peer reading, content area reading/writing, word study, or fluency work. Some teachers have mandatory activities that must be completed by the end of the week, but if a child would like to spend the majority of his or readers' workshop reading silently from a chosen text, he always have the option to do so. Primary grades may use a similar model where students move around to literacy centers. Nothing but reading/writing is done during the literacy block.

Table 3.5.   Example of Menu for Readers'/Writers' Workshop

	Weekly Menu
Name_____	Week of_____
Activity	Date Completed
___Silent reading	Every Day
___Vocabulary work	_____
___Word study work	_____
___Social studies_____	_____
___Science_____	_____
___Writing_____	
___Buddy reading	

STREAMLINING GUIDED READING

As districts begin to place more emphasis on reading success, principals may need to shift the way they have traditionally set up teachers' schedules to include designated blocks of time set aside for literacy and math. The principals of some of the schools utilizing this program have experimented and found success with a type of block scheduling; it is a minimum of sixty minutes of uninterrupted instructional time dedicated solely to literacy.

Teachers may bristle at the thought of being told when to teach what, but the benefits outweigh the autonomy they surrender. Realizing that all professionals work more efficiently when they work in holonomy, they respect the schedule, knowing that their students will receive what they need during the common time. The outcome of this model means greater flexibility for both reading intervention blocks and guided reading grouping.

For example, if the second grade teachers all teach their focus lesson from 9:30 to9:45, it becomes possible for reading support personnel to create their groups within all the classrooms at that grade. It also means that second-grade teachers can flexibly mix their guided reading groups based on reading levels across the grade level. One teacher may only have two children reading at level *K* while she has eight students at level *M*. Her neighbor next door has three students at level *K* and one at level *M*. These teachers have the option to consider sharing their students for guided reading because their reading workshop time is the same.

This goes for the students below grade level, as well. The support staff takes children across the grade level, based on their reading level to form intervention groups. No longer are support staff members "assigned" to a classroom teacher. Their groups are formed with a variety of students from different classrooms reading at the same level. We found that over the years this model works well for some schools and teachers while for others (due to classroom/school dynamics and logistics), it does not. The path each school takes is based on the needs of its students.

WORD STUDY/VOCABULARY INSTRUCTION

Because word study is a relatively new format of spelling instruction, most teachers did not experience this method as a student, nor as a preservice teacher. The majority of practicing teachers in our district typically were given a prescribed list of words to practice and memorize for Friday's spelling test. Most often, the entire class had the same lists and were given the same set of activities to work on, consisting of writing sentences with the words, looking them up in the dictionary, and so on. The assigned spelling lists did not reflect students' true abilities.

Learning complex vocabulary words most likely came in the form of content area work where in the textbook relevant words were introduced and found in bold print throughout the chapter. They were relevant at that time of learning but were soon forgotten because they did not really fit into the day-to-day life of an eight-year-old.

Hopefully, in today's classrooms, this method of spelling and vocabulary instruction has taken the same road as the dunce cap. We now recognize the developmental continuum of orthography learning and we capitalize on that knowledge to create word lists that will have the most impact on our students' ability. Kids need just-right books to read and appropriate words to spell at their level.

When the teachers of this program set out to reform the way in which reading and writing were taught, they looked at the importance of differentiating spelling instruction. In fact, no longer was it simply about spelling the words, it evolved into the actual study of the word, therefore referring to it as "word study." Structural analysis, word families, irregular spelling patterns, and so on, are all included in learning how to spell a word.

Students work with lists of words that include a principle of the week, high frequency words, and words that they have misspelled in their writing. They are given activities throughout the week that go beyond just using the words in sentences, but most important, students learn about words that are appropriate to their level.

As early as first grade, all students learn Greek and Latin affixes and root words. They use analytic and synthetic phonics strategies, depending on the complexity of the words. Because the words are always presented within a big picture, students are more easily able to connect a specific word that they are learning with others they may encounter. The spelling patterns are concretized and transferred into daily life. Word study is a purposeful way to teach children how to spell.

Although children do not need to spell the words they learn through vocabulary instruction, they are required to learn, utilize, and develop their vocabulary. About ten words per week are introduced from kindergarten to eighth grade. They are a combination of words we see and use in day-to-day life as well as words in students' content area instruction.

Going beyond just definitions, some of these words require a teaching of the concept done through picture cards that show the word in action or by the teacher asking a student to act out the word. For instance, a second-grade class may have the word *perseverance*. Students will be given the definition as well as a picture of the word in order to make a better connection. They will be asked to use it in a sentence as well as notice it in daily conversation or their reading.

SUMMARY

This is but one example of a comprehensive, home-grown literacy program that is based around research–based best practices. The structure is predicated on the readers'/writers' workshop and, although the emphasis here is placed more on reading, the writing component should follow the same structure—focus lesson, independent/guided writing, and wrap-up. Teachers are charged with deciding how to implement the grade-level standards, match their instruction with the needs and learning styles of their students, and follow research–based best practices.

Central to the design of the program is full buy-in by the administration. A design team predominantly made up of teachers cannot implement a program they believe to be effective if the administration does not understand and support the reasons behind it. This does not mean, however, that structured instruction gives way to arbitrariness simply because the teachers designed the curriculum, scope and sequence, and perhaps even the schedule.

If teachers feel as though they are given too much freedom, teacher empowerment may eventually lead to teaching that is too "loose," resulting in a sense of mistrust and anxiety felt by the administrators in the district. The parameters of the program must be balanced, giving equal weight to autonomy and accountability.

Chapter Four

"Facilitating" Change

SNAPSHOT #4

For the first time in the history of the school district, the role of "instructional leader" was under a bit of scrutiny. This did not imply that principals were incapable of providing their staff with meaningful leadership, or that they were unable to successfully perform the duties traditional to the role, it simply meant that within each building, there were others who possessed a level of expertise that was of equal value. This notion began to challenge what we have come to expect of our principals regardless of their experience or educational background.

Although a person is assigned the role of principal, they do not necessarily have the level of expertise needed to evaluate, guide, or even suggest ways to improve one's practice in all subject areas. Born from this idea was the Principal's Literacy Boot Camp. All principals attended a workshop day in the summer that was put on by the curriculum coordinator and literacy facilitators to discuss all things having to do with literacy.

The principals left that day with an abundance of information about readers'/writers' workshops, guided reading, word study, vocabulary instruction, just-right books, and so on. They felt empowered, while the literacy facilitators believed that they had begun to forge a productive new partnership that would support their teachers and program.

There is an abundance or research suggesting that student learning is directly influenced by teacher knowledge. It is unlikely that any curriculum or instructional program can sustain itself or demonstrate positive outcomes without some level of professional development. Unfortunately, in some districts, this crucial learning link is absent.

Superintendent Jean Briggs-Badger suggests that many school districts have it backwards. She believes that during teacher-led reading reform, the district invests in knowledge instead of "stuff." She further explains that when a district buys a basal, or core curriculum, they buy materials and supplements with professional development; however, when districts create their own reading curriculum, funds go into professional development and they supplement with materials.

Collaborative approaches to professional development, such as literacy coaching, have enjoyed an upsurge in the past decade as school systems respond to research reflecting a progression to more "andragogical" views of professional learning. The andragogical approach to professional development suggests that adults (in this case, teachers) learn differently from children and should be offered different opportunities to learn from what has been the norm in schools.

A coaching model of professional development is grounded in the belief that learning is constructed and socially mediated. A new role, that of the literacy facilitator, is proposed in this chapter. This position is intended to support and extend implementation of a home-grown curriculum and serves as the cornerstone for alignment, rigor, and quality.

We will further examine the necessity behind this role for instructional reform to occur whether in a home-grown program or not. We will discuss how the role of literacy coach and reading specialist contribute to this unique position and illustrate how the job description responds to the needs of the school/district and works with the resources available. In a teacher-created reading program, the goal is to reform the way in which the instruction is delivered to children. This modification process includes challenging long-held assumptions of how teachers, principals, paraprofessionals, reading specialists, and literacy coaches collaborate.

In 2004, the International Reading Association (IRA) suggested that the duties and qualifications of a literacy coach require them to:

• Be excellent teachers of reading—particularly at the levels in which they are assigned;
• Have in-depth knowledge of reading processes, acquisition, assessment, and instruction;
• Have expertise in working with teachers to improve their practices;
• Be excellent presenters and group leaders; and
• Have the experience or preparation that enables them to model, observe, and provide feedback about instruction for the classroom teacher (IRA, 2004).

As the No Child Left Behind Act of 2001 gained momentum, educational reform began to focus heavily on the way in which reading instruction was conceptualized and delivered in the United States. In many schools today, the reading specialist typically focuses on the assessment and remediation of children with reading difficulties. More recently, reform has morphed into a form that encompasses the needs of teachers as well.

In many schools, this happened by default simply because the reading specialist has always been viewed as an "expert" in literacy instruction. Often, the training for this position was lacking, but the expectations for this person remained high. She was expected to diagnose and remediate the learning needs of students and the pedagogical needs of teachers.

Time has passed and in many districts, the role of literacy coach has become a necessary element in educational reform. Extensive professional development opportunities, literature, and even college classes now exist highlighting the skills of a coach as the position evolves. State and federal legislation, along with district administrators, have begun to realize the benefits that come from such a position and how the role of coach differs from that of a reading specialist.

Since the IRA's position statement on literacy coaches in 2004, the guiding principles of this role have been better articulated and duties more clearly defined. In *Literacy Coaching—The Essentials* (2006), Katherine Casey outlines the requirements of a coach as:

- to help design and facilitate professional development sessions tailored to address issues facing teachers and students;
- to work alongside teachers in classrooms, demonstrating instructional strategies and guiding teachers as they try on the strategies;
- to evaluate students' literacy needs and collaborate with teachers to design instruction to meet those needs; and
- to provide teachers with ongoing opportunities to learn from and with each other.

In Mary Catherine Moran's *Differentiated Literacy Coaching—Scaffolding for Student and Teacher Success* (2007), she conceptualizes a framework that designates precisely where and how the coach will target the professional development needs of the teachers in their buildings. In her literacy coaching continuum, she identifies eight key areas of professional development that the coach will provide:

1. collaborative resource management
2. literacy content presentations
3. focused classroom visits
4. coplanning
5. study groups

6. demonstration lessons
7. peer coaching
8. coteaching

In a home-grown literacy program, the position of literacy coach is sub-sumed in the role of literacy facilitator. Many of the duties remain similar to that of the traditional coach; however, a greater emphasis is placed on the facilitation of the program and the teachers' responses to the demands of the curriculum. The role of facilitator encompasses all that the IRA, Casey, and Moran outlined, but it also requires, to a great extent, a more clearly defined leadership role. Let us first take a look at how the literacy facilitator is inte-gral to the flow of the program.

THE MANY RELATIONSHIPS
AND ROLES OF THE LITERACY FACILITATOR

Program Coordinator

Since the program is constantly evolving, it is imperative for the design team to meet regularly. This means that teachers from each building must collabo-rate with efficiency and effectiveness in order to make the changes necessary for the success of the program. As all educators know, once the school year is in full swing, time is at a premium. Teachers cannot be expected to leave their classrooms for extended periods of time, nor can most school districts afford the cost of substitutes as teachers write and modify curriculum.

In addition, few teachers welcome the added responsibility of committee work after the school day has ended. At that end, though, both need to occur if a home-grown program is to be successful. The program cannot survive or sustain itself without constant feedback from practitioners, so when they do collaborate, the time spent together is purposeful and well-planned. A human resource integral to the program's evolution is the literacy facilitator.

Meeting regularly, the district's literacy facilitators process the needs behind the scenes, performing the legwork necessary for the design team to delve into the work when they have the opportunity to come together. This may require some decision making by the facilitators so that goals can be set before the design team meets for its next work session. This is not to suggest that the literacy facilitators make unilateral decisions. It does mean that they discuss and assess the needs of the teachers in their assigned buildings.

Because they are living and breathing the program with those teachers at their building, they are able to brainstorm effective alternatives to present to all teachers when they meet as a team. Chances are, the issues experienced in one building are also experienced at another. Therefore, the literacy facilitator's role with respect to program facilitation is dual purpose—coordinate all teachers of literacy within their building, as well as co-coordinate all teachers of literacy across the district.

For consistency and continuity between all schools to be assured, it is essential that each building be represented by one person whose responsibility is to be a collective voice speaking on behalf of the teachers in their building. Without this component, instruction is fragmented and the program will lack reliability.

Personnel Coordinator

At the high-school level, most departments are led by a department chair. The person in this role acts as an instructional leader for that subject. Concerns with curriculum, instruction, and assessment are usually brought to this person and supported by the principal. It is now becoming more common to find a literacy coach and a math coach in a building or shared between schools, but these positions are not concrete fixtures in all district budgets. In a teacher-created literacy program, the budget must allow for the position of literacy facilitator as a mainstay.

It must be made clear that the literacy facilitator's supervisory role is not that of a principal. However, he may be asked to observe lessons being taught or sit in on the administering of a reading assessment; the information gleaned from that time is used for two purposes: 1) to ensure the success of students engaged in the program and 2) to support and scaffold classroom teachers' knowledge and learning in literacy instruction.

Similar to a coach, the literacy facilitator may engage in pre- and post-observation meetings with the teacher. Together, they may plan objectives and focus questions as the literacy facilitator scaffolds the teacher through her learning process, but unlike those of a principal, the areas of concern are never formalized through any form of documentation. Anything written down stays between the facilitator and the teacher.

The principal respects the process and understands that confidentiality between the two parties is sacred. When the literacy facilitator enters a classroom, it is without judgment or threat. A breach of this trust would simply destroy the framework that is vital to the success of the program.

In terms of personnel, the literacy facilitator answers to four parties. The relationship he fosters with each party is exclusive, yet the success of each is crucial if students are to flourish academically. Figure 4.1 shows the exclusivity and the interconnectedness.

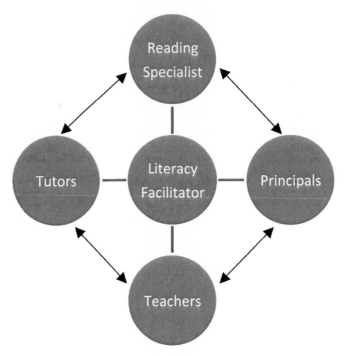

Figure 4.1.   The Various Relationships of the Literacy Facilitator

Literacy Facilitator/Tutor Relationship

The function of tutor/paraprofessional is included in the design of a home-grown program. Most schools are afforded limited resources in terms of personnel, but in most cases there is, to some extent, a level of support staff that exists in a building. If used judiciously, the power of the paraprofessional can be limitless, but this does not come without recognizing that they, too, require ongoing learning opportunities if they are expected to do work similar to that of the classroom teachers.

Professional development opportunities given to the teachers by way of PD funds are not always available to support staff. Oftentimes paraprofessionals are as excited and eager to learn best practices alongside the classroom teachers, but due to budgetary constraints they are excluded. As part of the PD design in a teacher-created program, the paraprofessional is included in the dissemination of instructional knowledge and methods. They are encouraged to address their areas of need with the literacy facilitator and invited to take advantage of professional development opportunities within the district.

If they are asked to run guided reading groups in conjunction with the classroom teachers, then they must be trained in the practice of guided reading. If the classroom teachers plan on using their assessment data for reporting purposes, it is imperative that the paraprofessional know the proper protocol for administering a reading assessment.

In order for schools to maximize the invaluable resources they have within their buildings, they must be willing to set aside time and promote the professional development framework that is set up for their support staff. The literacy facilitator–paraprofessional relationship link may be one of the less obvious in terms of curriculum coordination; however, it is one of the strongest components in the program's infrastructure. The power of the school support staff should never be underestimated, nor should it be underutilized.

Literacy Facilitator/Reading Specialist Relationship

For the most part, a reading specialist's background, experience, and education are equivalent to that of the literacy facilitator. Through the reform efforts we are speaking of, the roles take on exclusive characteristics. The reading specialist sees children either in small groups or one on one. She may coordinate services with special education or Title I, but her primary role is as interventionist.

Through diagnosis and remediation of reading difficulties, the reading specialist's role is vital in implementing the intervention portion of the program. Also, classroom teachers may solicit the help of the reading specialist for guided reading/writing groups, whether to model best practices or to take groups during the reading/writing workshop. The specialist may be asked to provide enrichment for higher level students or provide reteaching opportunities after a common formative assessment is analyzed. The literacy facilitator aids in the coordination of such processes.

The reading specialist and literacy facilitator are in constant contact, often sharing the same work space and meeting regularly throughout the week. Their collaboration ensures that the program runs as efficiently as possible. Since both are in most classrooms regularly, they can guide one another to where each other's expertise could be most beneficial.

For example, if the literacy facilitator is modeling a series of lessons for a second grade teacher and notices a child whose comprehension skills are lacking, she can guide the reading specialist to that student. Conversely, if the reading specialist runs a guided reading group in a classroom and notices gaps in a teacher's literacy instruction, she can guide the literacy facilitator to that classroom. Because the combined knowledge base of the literacy facilitator and reading specialist is boundless, the potential for instructional reform in literacy is limitless.

Literacy Facilitator–Classroom Teacher Relationship

John Dewey writes in *Democracy in Education* (1916):

> There is more than a verbal tie between the words common, community, and communication. Men live in a community in virtue of the things which they have in common; and communication is the way in which they come to possess things in common. What they must have in common in order to form a community or society are aims, beliefs, aspirations, knowledge—a common understanding—like-mindedness as the sociologists say. Such things cannot be passed physically from one to another, like bricks; they cannot be shared as persons would share a pie by dividing it into physical pieces. The communication which insures participation in a common understanding is one which secures similar emotional and intellectual dispositions—like ways of responding to expectations and requirements. (p.8)

The relationship between the literacy facilitator and classroom teacher is grounded in communication. Instructional reform cannot occur, nor can it sustain existence, in an environment where teachers are coerced into believing in the efficacy of a particular program. Instead, they must be guided, educated, and invited to bring with them their own philosophy of how children learn best so they can explore how the program can be used as a guide and tool to complement their own pedagogical understandings.

The literacy facilitator must be mindful of the fact that all teachers, even the newest, bring with them a cache of knowledge that cannot be ignored or replaced. What each teacher brings to the table is just as important as what the program offers them. When the two are combined, teaching is at its best.

One of the literacy facilitator's duties is to foster the communication that Dewey promoted. The facilitator finds ways to support all viewpoints and best practices while promoting every teacher's participation in the desire to understand how children learn. He creates an environment where teachers are asked to experiment with strategic problem solving so that when success is achieved the empowerment felt by the teachers drives them to persist and to share their successes with others. Their ownership in the program evolves over time because they have a say in how teaching looks in their classroom.

This is grounded in Dewey's (1938) theory of the transactional process and Vygotsky's (1978) zone of proximal development. Both are steeped in the belief that through active participation and scaffolding, learners are able to move confidently from the unknown to the known. Although this concept is usually connected to student learning, teachers working with the literacy facilitator find themselves learning through inquiry alongside their students.

Teachers as learners eventually become teacher-leaders as they construct and test new ideas. Teachers actively construct knowledge through an integration of the world and their personal experiences (Knowles, 1980). This runs counter to the expectations of a prepackaged prescribed reading program, where the teacher is expected to transmit knowledge from an unknown entity.

Another component to the relationship between classroom teacher and literacy facilitator is the ability to spread insight and discovery throughout the building. The literacy facilitator is the instructional lifeline between the classrooms. All teachers are encouraged by the facilitator to contribute to the betterment of the program by sharing their methods with all parties involved in the school's learning community.

Although the literacy facilitator's main objective is to ensure the teacher's effectiveness in the program's implementation, a level of reciprocity exists that fortifies the program. The literacy facilitator learns from the classroom teacher just as the opposite occurs. Because she is present in classrooms around the school and across the district, she is able to see literacy instruction through a broader lens and can easily disseminate the variety of approaches she observes others using in addition to her own.

For example, if a third-grade teacher has devised an efficient way to balance time between individual reading conferences and guided reading groups, that teacher may be asked to model her approach in other classrooms or be observed by fellow teachers who are looking for a way to more effectively differentiate reading instruction. Another option is for the literacy facilitator to spend time observing the practice and later bring the approach into other classrooms, proliferating effective instruction across the district.

Literacy Facilitator–Principal Relationship

As reform movements gain momentum and school improvement plans require representation from a variety of district employees, the traditional leadership paradigm is being challenged. In some school districts, principals are solely responsible for upwards of five hundred children, and a staff of fifty to seventy-five. As previously mentioned, this challenge is most apparent at the elementary level where department heads are not a part of the typical K-5 budget.

Out of necessity, instructional leadership has taken a backseat while management has moved to the forefront. It is impossible and unfair to expect the principal to be an "expert" in all areas of teaching. It is challenging enough for reading specialists to stay abreast of changing trends in early-literacy instruction while understanding all that is entailed in delivering differentiated instruction to the wide span of developmental needs of elementary students and they study such practices.

In an age of data-driven decision making, building principals do not have the time to pore over reading/writing assessment scores with the hope of matching the most effective intervention to a child's needs. A savvy administrator understands that although decision and policy making have their home at the central office, teachers are the final decision makers when it comes to instructional practices, since they are at the learning environment's ground zero—the classroom.

Based on Gamoran and Porter's (1994) research that found student achievement is directly linked to teacher control over curricular content, Katzenmeyer and Moller (2001) assert that teachers should always be included in the "hows" of instructional practice. Constraints due to state and national standards may hinder decisionmaking with respect to the "what" of curriculum but it is imperative that the power of a teacher and the knowledge of the subject area do not go underappreciated.

Spillane and Harris's (2006) idea of a distributed perspective, where the management and leadership of a school go far beyond the capacity of a principal, runs parallel to the leadership philosophy of a teacher-created program. Although the principals are very active participants in the execution of the curriculum, the role they play is that of supporter rather than manager. The principal is a partner with the literacy facilitator, placing most of the leadership for curriculum, instructional methods, and professional development as it relates to literacy in the hands of the facilitator.

Regardless of background, experience, or depth of knowledge, it is imperative that the principals of a district regularly attend design meetings, assist in curriculum and lesson writing, and stay abreast of necessary program changes or evolving needs of the teachers. They are integral in the decision making, but the principal does not exercise exclusivity when it comes to coordinating literacy instruction within the building. The principal and literacy facilitator must remain in constant contact.

In a teacher-created literacy program, the model promotes the notion that it takes more than one instructional leader to coordinate and implement a rigorous reading and writing curriculum. Because of his years of experience, education, and background in literacy instruction, it is the literacy facilitator's intellectual capital that weighs heavily in the balance of power and affords him the skills necessary to share the instructional leadership with the principal.

Hersey and Natemeyer's (1979) work with power types illustrates the two types of power existing in an organization—positional and personal. It is the personal power base that directly correlates to the position of the literacy facilitator within a school.

Grounded in the belief that the power he possesses is based solely on his actions (as opposed to positional power that is granted by a central office), he is better able to lead classroom teachers due to his ability to connect to them as practitioners. His capacity to develop and strengthen the program *with* them through a shared vision is where his leadership is most effective. He may practice one or all of the three types of power that Hersey and Natemeyer established in their Power Base Perception model:

1. Referent power—she has classroom teaching experience and can model a variety of effective instructional strategies, making her relatable to the average classroom teacher. She understands the daily ins and outs of teaching reading and writing. She can walk the walk and talk the talk.
2. Information power—she is an invaluable resource to teachers of literacy. She attends professional development opportunities and brings that information back to the classroom teachers.
3. Expert power—she has experience focusing exclusively on best practices in literacy instruction. She is an in-house expert at the teachers' fingertips. (Katzenmeyer & Moller, 2001)

Because a teacher-created program is grounded in the democratic model, no one in the building is coerced or forced to adhere to specific requirements when it comes to *how* they deliver their instruction. It is just the opposite. Teachers are encouraged to mold and shape the program in a way that best suits their students' learning as well as their own teaching styles.

But because their concentration on teaching the nonnegotiable standards, they will be held accountable by the administration. Fortunately, the literacy facilitator is there to provide guidance and support for teachers and principals.

Literacy Walk-Through

It is unrealistic to expect a principal with little or no background in literacy instruction to effectively evaluate a teacher on his methods of instruction. Perhaps the principal was a math teacher in her past and has little knowledge of phonological awareness or how to demonstrate voice in a narrative. Here is where the shared leadership is most imperative.

The recurring literacy walk-through is built into the structure of a teacher-created program (see figure 4.2). Informal, yet informational, it provides the literacy facilitator and principal with a glimpse into the daily workings of a literacy-based classroom. The observations are brief and nonjudgmental, and conducted initially by the literacy facilitator and the principal together.

The purpose of the walk-through is multifaceted. First and foremost, it provides the facilitators with an on-site, big-picture view of the workings of each teacher's literacy block. When conducting a walk-through, the literacy facilitator is honing in on specific items crucial to successful literacy instruction. For the principal, the walk-throughs serve a different purpose. It is their turn to be a student of the literacy curriculum.

LITERACY WALK-THROUGH

Classroom_____
Date/Time_____
Observer_____

*Teachers are in no way expected to demonstrate evidence of every component on this form. The walk-through is intended to last 15–20 minutes and observations are based only on what has been seen during that time. The observer will place a check near the component of the reader's workshop indicating when he/she was in the classroom.

Focus Lesson _____
- Lesson is connected to standard and "I can" statements
- Length of focus lesson is appropriate (approx. 10–15 min.)
- Teacher modeling is apparent
- Students have an opportunity for quick guided practice

Independent Reading _____
- Students are engaged in text or literacy activity
- Students are able to select a book appropriate to their level and articulate why
- Students are able to select books with efficiency and choose from a wide variety of genres
- Students can articulate what the focus lesson is and provide an example

Guided Reading _____
- Instruction is differentiated and individualized based on student needs
- Group size corresponds to instructional needs of students
- Students are reading leveled texts based on their abilities
- Teacher focuses on reading skill(s)
- E.g. rereading for meaning, using context clues, word work, etc.

Materials and Supplies _____
- Students have ample reading materials from which to choose
- Classroom library is well organized with a large variety of genres and leveled text
- Teacher has appropriate materials with which to teach (mentor texts, easel, chart paper, etc.)

A noteworthy moment:

Comments:

Figure 4.2.   Literacy Walk-Through Form

Finally, for the teacher, walk-throughs provide specific and immediate feedback on the holonomy level across teachers. Are the lessons increasing in rigor as the grade levels rise? Are mentor texts offering new and different insights as a student grows?

Ahead of time, teachers may ask the literacy facilitator to pay close attention to specific aspects of the readers' or writers' workshop and to look for gaps or overlaps in instruction. After a series of walk-throughs are conducted, the literacy facilitators across the district begin to analyze the data in order to find flaws in the program or to move forward with professional development opportunities that might be needed district-wide.

In addition, the walk-through is used to inform the principal. For the ten to fifteen minutes the principal is observing literacy instruction, he is taking notes and paying close attention to various components of instruction. He will then debrief with the literacy facilitator once the walk-through is complete, ask questions, clarify misconceptions, and build his knowledge of best practices in reading and writing.

The walk-through form never enters the classroom teacher's file and it is not used as an evaluation tool. It educates the principal enough so that when a formal observation occurs during the literacy block, the principal is well informed and familiar with the components of instruction. The evaluation becomes purposeful and relevant for the teacher and principal.

Through this symbiotic relationship between principal and literacy facilitator, schools can avoid Elmore's assertion that 'it is easy to make mistakes in judgment about better or worse teaching, and it is particularly easy to make egregious mistakes when those who make the judgments know little about what constitutes expert practice" (2002, p. 26). He goes on to say, "in most systems, the administrators who are assigned the responsibility for evaluating teachers are not selected for the expertise in instruction; indeed, most of their work has nothing to do with instruction. So it's not surprising that teachers distrust principals for individual assessment of their quality and competence" (p. 26).

When teachers perceive the principal is evaluating based on incomplete or inaccurate judgments, this process offers little room for the teacher to improve her practice. Because one of the major reasons for a walk-through is the education of the *principal*, teachers are more apt to accept their evaluations with a more open mind. When teachers become used to seeing their principal in the classroom, they begin to consider her as a working, collegial partner in the education of their students, rather than as a supervisor looking for something that should be improved.

Trust is crucial. If the classroom teachers truly believe the objective of the principal's observation is to understand the workings of a literacy-based classroom, they begin to trust that the intent of the observations is to focus on student outcomes, not classroom management or teaching style.

All classroom teachers know that the literacy facilitator will guide and inform the principal throughout the process and any aspect of their teaching that could use improvement will be targeted through professional development rather than be noted on an evaluation form and placed in the teacher's file. As long as teachers remain confident that their areas of improvement become learning opportunities rather than judgments, the relationships among the teacher, principal, and literacy facilitator continually enrich the program.

Systemic instructional reform is a result of this shift in thinking. The traditional structure of the school is not simply changed, but rather the instructional infrastructure of the school is "recultured" (Hargreaves and Fullan 1998). The transformation is grounded in the idea that all stakeholders are equal members of a learning community, and through collaborative efforts, student learning is the focus, rather than teacher performance. Principals can be effective instructional leaders instead of merely managing a staff through intimidating evaluations and power brandishing.

A principal who exercises dynamic leadership seeks out leaders among her staff and encourages them to become vanguards in the reform process. Principals who are engaged in real school change recognize that every teacher can be a leader in partnership with the principal and that the role of teaching, learning, and leading can be played by everyone (Katzenmeyer and Moller, 2001). In a teacher-created literacy program, the literacy facilitator can assist in identifying those teachers who are leaders in literacy instruction and direct the principal to them.

BOTTOM-UP LEADERSHIP

Reforming reading instruction by way of a teacher-designed curriculum requires participation and buy-in from all stakeholders but also requires strong leadership. No longer can one person, traditionally the principal, be responsible for determining all of the needs of all staff members. Designated experts in each discipline can better assess the needs of the teachers and determine the professional development path for them.

With respect to literacy, in a teacher-designed program, the literacy facilitator takes on the role of educational leader, while classroom teachers whose knowledge is strong in the area of literacy aid in providing job-embedded professional development. Lipsky (1980) calls them "Street Level Bureaucrats"—the people on the ground floor living and breathing curriculum while inadvertently driving education reform.

Lipsky believed that because public service employees (in this case the teachers) make daily decisions, create routines, and learn to cope with the demands and uncertainties of the profession, ostensibly they become the policy makers. Policy is written and solidified in the corner offices or by the legislative bodies, but it is the way in which employees on the ground floor react, respond, and service the needs of their constituents (the students) that drives the decision makers to write and enact policy. In a sense, they are classroom bureaucrats.

A collective voice is a powerful one. Often in education, we witness such change when a new reading or math program is adopted either school-wide or district-wide. For the most part, classroom teachers will implement the program with the requisite fidelity should they find the program's elements to be sound instructionally and to meet the needs of their students as well as their own pedagogical beliefs.

Once a teacher or two in a building begins to lose faith in the program, the bandwagon mentality occurs as others feel free to voice their dissatisfaction with the program. From there, a variety of situations can take place, leading ultimately to a systematic change in program, be it school-wide or district-wide. In some cases, the teachers simply choose to "shelve" the program altogether as they resort to their own methods.

Although program adoption is not a policy enactment per se, the ability of a group of teachers to effectuate change is an example of Lipsky's theory of how street-level bureaucrats are able to influence systemic decision making. It is wise and confident administrators who listen and respond to the concerns of their employees.

When teachers' collective voices go unheard, it is to the detriment of the students. A once cohesive, unified school/district now opens its doors to distrust and fragmentation; in the end, instruction suffers. For any kind of instructional reform to take place in education, whether in literacy, science, or math, crucial to the reform is the partnership between the decision makers/ policy writers and the classroom bureaucrats.

Marzano, Waters, and McNulty (2005) believe that through coordinated actions set forth by the administration, a plan of improvement that includes a leadership team rather than one person assuming the role of leader results in student achievement. They assert that when a purposeful community is created and a shared vision is established, all teachers focus their instruction to meet that goal. One of the by-products of a teacher-created literacy program is the shared vision and instructional focus that come when a group of educators in a building or district see themselves as equal members of a community, all contributing to the achievement of a common goal.

This idea of a shared community does not imply harmony and acquiescence among the community members. In fact, it is likely that instructional reform is achieved with some degree of friction and discomfort. For some, stepping out of the classroom is a welcome opportunity for growth, while for others, it is threatening. All communities require a variety of voices, both loud and quiet in order for change to occur, and this realization is the first step toward collective efficacy. The members who provide support are equally important to the leaders in the community. There is some level of participation from all educators in the district.

This cooperation runs parallel to what the 2007 (Brinson and Steiner) issue brief from The Center for Comprehensive School Reform and Improvement purported with respect to collective teacher efficacy mentioned in chapter 1. In a study (Pfaff 2000) of a small group of teachers who were engaged in a self-directed professional study, it was found that those teachers who had already possessed high levels of perceived efficacy maintained those attitudes throughout the course of the school year, as opposed to peers who did not take part in the study group. In fact, nonmembers demonstrated significant decreases in perceived efficacy. The study concluded that principals can sustain perceptions of collective teacher efficacy, even in the smallest of capacities and with the most limited resources, as long as they are willing to support innovative efforts put forth by the teachers in their building.

The brief goes on to include the work of Goddard, Hoy, and Hoy (2004), who assert that if teachers are given occasions to be influential when it comes to making instructionally based decisions, it is probable that collective efficacy will continue. Teachers who feel effective and are invited to contribute to curriculum development, purchasing of materials, and professional development opportunities go on to feel a sense of professional nourishment and self-worth. Simply put, they strive to be successful practitioners.

The process is unpredictable. Teachers as contributing leaders come in varying degrees. We found in our experience that as the notion of a teacher-created literacy program became a reality, leaders emerged organically. A formalized team was not created. A variety of teachers came forth on their own in order to be a part of the process. These were teachers who, a) had backgrounds in reading and writing instruction, b) knew little about literacy and looked to better their instructional practice, and/or c) were interested in being a part of the decision-making process.

No single teacher was asked by the administration to be a member of the design team but anyone interested was welcomed. All teachers district-wide were notified of the process and encouraged to join the committee. After a series of committee meetings took place and the groundwork was established, outlining the expectations for the team, some team members stayed while others took a break. From there, a leadership team developed organically and it remains this way throughout the years.

It is important to keep in mind that, although the original design-team members continue to take a front seat in terms of the literacy leadership across the district, others who are less vocal are continually encouraged to take part in the reform process. The team still evolves and reshapes itself each year, with some members stepping back and others coming forward, but the core of the design team remains solid. A program that is responsive is a living document and adjusts to the needs of the students and teachers as it maintains ongoing success.

SUMMARY

A district-wide literacy program that is the brainchild of teachers—these Street Level Bureaucrats—cannot be successfully implemented without the aid of a facilitator. Part of the reform process is to honor and capitalize on the expertise and experiences of *all* of the district's staff including principals, teachers, and paraprofessionals. All constituents from the principal to the tutors are encouraged to work closely with the literacy facilitator in order to support and develop knowledge of literacy instruction.

Through a distributed model of oversight, a principal shares her educational leadership with a literacy facilitator knowing that she will be more effective when it comes time to evaluate the program and support the teaching staff. Without judgment or formal evaluations, the literacy facilitator conducts objective observations independently or alongside the principal.

If literacy instruction is to be reformed, principals can no longer follow the standard protocol that has been handed down over the years. The change process requires a shared vision that invites all educators to take part in reaching that vision regardless of titles or status in the building.

Chapter Five

Investing in Knowledge

SNAPSHOT #5

Teacher in-service and early release days took on a whole new definition. No longer were teachers asked to listen to an outside consultant (perhaps someone who had been out of the classroom for too long to remember what it was like in the trenches), or given tasks that appeared menial, keeping them from working productively in their rooms. Because their newly adopted, home-grown literacy program was the product of the teachers in the district, everyone was asked to work toward its completion during the professional development days.

This was a leap of faith for the administrators and a welcomed change for most K–8 teachers. They spent time collaborating with colleagues across the district and within their schools to write lessons that were relevant, targeting *their* students. Driven by the district's literacy facilitators, teachers were inspired to write curricula that would be used by their peers. They were careful, methodical, and at the end, proud of what they had accomplished. It was collegial collaboration at its finest. And, there was no financial cost to the district.

A 2007 study examining the world's twenty-five best-performing schools suggests teacher quality as the main driver of student achievement (McKinsey 2007). If we act on what the research intimates, it is not enough that a district implement a quality curriculum, it is also imperative that school districts strengthen and expand the knowledge, skills, and resourcefulness of their teachers. Reforms such as the one we describe are not self-implementing, nor consistently implemented as intended. To carry out curricular implementation effectively, teachers need high-quality professional development.

Sadly, and at the detriment of our students, this information has been slow to affect the way professional development is conducted in schools. Hunt (2009) observes that "professional learning in its current state is poorly conceived and deeply flawed" (Foreword, Darling-Hammond et al. 2009). These flaws are attributed in part to a lack of time and opportunity to engage with and learn from colleagues; however, teachers continue to be required to attend "episodic, myopic and often meaningless" training (Hunt 2009).

As solo practitioners, teachers spend most of their day in isolation from their peers. Few educators are given opportunities for collegial conversation and collaboration within the school day. Many teachers only have their planning periods or lunch time to learn from one another or share ideas. In some schools, it may be considered a luxury to have an entire grade level sent off to a workshop together or to invite a paid consultant or professional trainer to come into a school and work with teachers in their buildings. But why should this be considered a luxury? Why are teachers working in isolation when their day is spent building a community of learners?

One recurring, overarching answer to these questions is funding. School districts often do not have the resources they need to provide their teachers with carefully thought out, purposeful professional development intended for the betterment of the entire staff rather than just a few members, but a lack of money can sometimes cause people to act in ways that are unexpected. A lack of funds can drive creative people to tap into ingenuity they never imagined they possessed, rather than concede to the status quo, ultimately leading to positive reform. A teacher-designed literacy program is one example of that positive reform.

Since a home-grown curriculum is written by the district's employees already on the payroll, the majority of cash expenditures comes in the form of hiring substitutes to cover for classroom teachers while they collaborate with their peers or attend in-district, job-embedded professional development opportunities. Additional funding may be necessary for small stipends and resources. The program and its success is the result of the teachers' brainpower and a willingness on the part of the administration to support those teachers in the creative process. The teachers sustain the program as they implement it throughout the year.

To take this idea beyond mere conceptualization, we will use the school district that is highlighted throughout this book. When the district began exploring prepackaged, core reading programs, they were looking at upwards of $800,000 to outfit three elementary schools and one middle school. In addition, money would be spent on outsourcing professional development to enhance the program. Instead, the district spent approximately $300,000 on resources such as mentor texts, leveled classroom/bookroom libraries, professional texts, and so on. The district's literacy facilitators provide the majority of the professional development.

Furthermore, few resources purchased were consumables that needed replenishment each year—a considerable cost of keeping up a prepackaged, core program. Jean Briggs-Badger, Superintendent of Schools, observed that when a district purchases a basal (or core curriculum), they pay for materials and supplement with professional development. Conversely, what this district did was to pay for professional development and supplement with materials.

CLASSROOM TEACHERS AS DECISION MAKERS

Conscientious teachers are always mindful of their students' needs and because of this, differentiate their instruction knowing that a generic delivery of instruction is ineffective. Administrators have come to expect this level of proficiency within their teachers, as well. So, if teachers are required to differentiate their instruction based on the needs of their students, then their professional development should run parallel to that notion.

A linchpin to reforming literacy instruction lies within the knowledge base of the teacher. If a first-grade teacher is expected to tear off the cellophane of her new, core program, written for generic children in mind, then the professional development she receives with that program will also be generic. But when a first-grade teacher turns to a lesson that has been written with HER students in mind and backed with professional development based on HER needs, the teaching and learning are harmonious and effective.

No longer is she a solo practitioner left to her own devices in order to teach by way of a manual; she is now the cornerstone to a curriculum that is responsive to the needs of both teacher and students. Because the program she implements is dynamic in nature, the curriculum and the teaching flex and mold to the learners, not the opposite. There is a hitch to this. If we expect students to demonstrate competency on various local, state, and national assessments and teacher competency hinges on these outcomes, then a deal must be struck between the practitioners and the decision makers.

Elmore (Elmore in Elmore 2002, p. 5) refers to this deal as "reciprocity of accountability for capacity." In a quid pro quo fashion, if the stakeholders expect results, teachers must be afforded the tools necessary to accomplish the task. They must have the opportunity to voice their needs and be heard by those who have the ability to promote the change.

Teacher-led reform can only go so far. Teachers must be encouraged to ascertain and voice their needs knowing that they have full support of administration. How these needs are managed and addressed in a time-sensitive manner is, perhaps, the most significant part of the process, especially when resources are limited and capital continues to decline.

PROFESSIONAL DEVELOPMENT
WITH A SENSE OF URGENCY

Educators are advised to teach with a sense of urgency. This has become a common buzz phrase in the field of education. Professional learning communities focus on texts that inspire teachers and administrators to promote this ideology, but when there is little direction or few resources to sustain the excitement one feels upon finishing the text, then the urgency becomes a moot point; it remains an ideology rather than becoming a reality. People begin running without knowing where they are going.

Instructional reform by way of a teacher-designed literacy program is a start. Since the teachers are writing a student-centered, standards-driven curriculum, they are constantly mindful of their audience and how students will respond to the lessons they create. Teaching with urgency is replaced with teaching with a laser-like focus on targeted goals. Teachers can teach with a sense of urgency because they know what areas of learning need the most attention.

Transparency is essential for reform to occur. When all stakeholders (including the school board, parents, and community) are engaged in this instructional reform process, skepticism, distrust, and fear give way to proactive problem solving where classroom and office doors are open in order to discourage the typical knee-jerk reaction—throw money at it or call in the high-paid consultant.

A collective commitment fosters what Janis (1982) called "groupthink." This concept emphasizes the need to eliminate action that is thoughtless and wasteful. Through groupthink people engage in a mode of thinking where cohesion replaces unanimity, resulting in a new course of action. Members of this group constantly question the status quo while brainstorming and experimenting with ways to transform tired, ineffective instructional practices.

In a home-grown literacy program, no proposal is initially rejected. Instead, all teachers are encouraged to put their ideas on the table where others can question, analyze, or build upon them. This does not mean, though, that anything goes. For example, a brand-new teacher on the team may offer a way to better balance her guided reading groups with her tiered intervention groups. She may be confronted with a large number of group members who have taught far longer than she has and appear skeptical—these teachers may even present themselves as "experts" in that area. Two things must happen in this situation: the new teacher must prove her method is successful through evidence and examples of her success, while the more seasoned teachers must remain open-minded and willing to try this new method.

This process requires the experts to suspend judgments and assumptions while they re-evaluate their own methods that they have implemented year after year. Teacher-led reform requires teachers to step up or down, according to their level of experience, in order to meet at a common ground. But reform cannot happen unless all parties are willing to share and let go of past practices. Through this checks-and-balances system, decisions are made in the best interest of that district's student population. The new approach is tried and tested in designated classrooms before it is adopted and expected to be implemented.

By no means is this a quick process. Teachers and administrators must be assured that all decisions and expectations set forth are logical and steeped in best practice. This evolutionary process avoids Fullan's (in Hargreaves 2010) notion of inertia and promotes a more focused sense of urgency that propels progress. It promotes a fervent level of positive pressure that is powerful, yet sensitive. No one is strong-armed into transforming instructional practices. Instead, they are informed and given time to adjust to the new expectations through professional development.

DELIVERY OF KNOWLEDGE

Professional Development = Continuous Learning

It is highly unlikely that a mechanic learned how to work on a car by simply reading about it or watching someone take apart a transmission. It is also unlikely that she spent countless hours in a classroom listening to an instructor talk about the best ways to disassemble a catalytic converter. The majority of successful mechanics had a desire to tinker in the garage on their own. Quite possibly it took years of experience to master skills and develop efficiency to a point where it became a lucrative livelihood.

Furthermore, as technology evolves, so must a mechanic's knowledge base. By differentiating her knowledge, it becomes possible that she will be able to work on a brand-new Ford as well as a 1987 model. Ironically, mechanical know-how is the product of a hands-on, organic process.

This model should be no different from the way in which educators work. Years of college coursework alone cannot prepare a teacher for what he will experience in the classroom. In order to develop as a practitioner, a teacher must first be encouraged to strengthen his practice. It starts with the administration realizing that college coursework is merely a beginning, the foundation for a teacher's knowledge base.

McKinsey (2007) discovered that schools operating most effectively had defined what quality instruction looked like. They provided a "system of support" to give teachers tools they needed to deliver effective and reliable instruction no matter the day, time of year, or many other variables that can influence the learning environment from day to day.

It is not enough to merely have a district-wide teacher induction program implemented for new teachers or to rely on the teacher recertification process to keep seasoned teachers performing at their best. Administrators must guide and encourage their staff to seek out PD opportunities both as individuals and as collaborative groups. The knowledge they receive should then be distributed throughout the staff by way of professional learning environments both in class and out. As discussed in chapter 4, the bottom line is that administrators not only support this model, they encourage and become active participants in the process.

Learning Options for Teachers

Urgency hinges on the immediacy and access to resources (including human resources) that teachers have in order to perfect their craft. Effective and efficient teaching is better achieved if the implemented curriculum is so familiar to individuals *within* the building or district that questions are answered instantly and curriculum issues are addressed without delay. This is the basis of a teacher-designed literacy program. Without it, teachers would continue to teach in a vacuum where opportunities for growth only occur once or twice a year during an in-service day or during a workshop outside of the school.

In 1994, the National Education Commission on Time and Learning cited a RAND study that found that, when learning new teaching strategies, teachers needed upwards of fifty hours of instruction, practice, and coaching before becoming comfortable with them (1994). A typical teacher workshop usually lasts the same number of hours as a school day (six to seven hours), loading on most of the information in a matter of hours and expecting the attendees to go back to their schools and implement what they learned. Without the ongoing guidance and scaffolding one needs to confidently implement the new strategy, the recommended fifty hours of practice is merely a luxury.

In a home-grown literacy program where the professional development is built into the framework, one option is to provide teachers with a menu of learning opportunities (see table 5.1).

This dynamic menu is created based on the needs of the teachers and administrators and changes as needs change. It is presented by the literacy facilitator at the onset of the school year and can be adjusted as the year progresses. Through regular grade-level meetings, the facilitator touches

Table 5.1. Professional Development Menu

Please choose three PD opportunities and prioritize them in order of "urgency".

At the bottom of the form, please put down the best time to meet to discuss your schedule.

Teacher Name:	1, 2, 3
Observe literacy facilitator or reading specialist model a focus lesson	
Aid in facilitating intervention and guided reading groups	
Workshops for strengthening comprehension, decoding strategies, fluency, etc.	
Observe a series of Six Traits lessons	
How to set up and maintain a classroom library	
How to maximize the readers' workshop time	
Blend reading/writing with math	
Conduct a series of lessons on responding to reading	
Analyze the results of a reading assessment	
Form guided reading groups based on assessment results	
Observe colleague during readers'/writers' workshop	
Other suggestion:	

base with the classroom teachers to ensure the menu includes options that are useful to them. Figure 5.1 is an example of some teacher-facilitator items one might find on a PD menu:

Teachers let the literacy facilitator know what they need and the times that fit into their schedules. If a teacher is required to be out of the room for a period of time to observe a colleague, typically the literacy facilitator will cover the class for that teacher. Similar to the coaching model, the classroom teacher and facilitator meet one on one afterwards (or throughout, depending on the PD) to discuss, debrief, and answer any further questions.

The facilitator will also coordinate the observations between staff members. Certain teachers are highlighted by the literacy facilitator to be observed due to their areas of expertise. We have found that the teacher-to-teacher observations are excellent avenues to start professional development for a variety of reasons; one is the relatedness the visiting teacher feels to the colleague she is observing, for example. Both the observer and the observed perceive each other to be on a leveled playing field. Examples of teacher-to-teacher observations are:

- The administering of a reading assessment;
- Keeping a focus lesson to 10–15 minutes;
- One-on-one reading/writing conference; and
- Keeping the flow of the readers' workshop, particularly with the rotation of guided reading groups

EMBRACING THE DATA

Introspection is essential to becoming a mindful, purposeful teacher. Few humans are comfortable when it comes to facing shortcomings—the average teacher is no exception. Educators know their students look to them for answers and they risk great scrutiny from the public if they do not hold themselves to the highest standard possible. However, when classroom teachers are asked to meet the needs of individuals in crowded classrooms and ensure appropriate differentiation, it can seem like an insurmountable task. But the actual differentiation may not be the problem.

The problem lies within knowing where to differentiate. This means the teacher must have a clear understanding of which students require varying degrees of instruction, as well as what tools to use to determine the needs. Furthermore, individual needs fluctuate throughout the school year.

For example, as any teacher of reading knows, a child who possesses excellent decoding skills may not comprehend the text in a way that is commensurate with her accuracy. Conversely, a child who demonstrates poor fluency may be able to think and discuss critically the text she has just read. So how does a classroom teacher manage this on her own? Or does she?

With positive pressure, educators can better motivate one another to meet the needs of their diverse student population while achieving results. Together, teachers and administrators examine and discuss data if the data are transparent and the discourse is open, honest, and without judgment or consequences. Professionals connect positive results with strategic pedagogy while eliminating intimidation and competition between staff members.

This model of continuous open dialogue looks beyond the needs of the student and focuses on the needs of the teacher. "We have to be able to access and learn from others who are employing more effective instructional practices in getting greater achievement results with given groups of students" (Fullan 2010, p. 125)."

As mentioned in chapter 2, instructional reform is incomplete without accountability. Common formative assessments that are given after a series of lessons shed light into a child's understanding of a concept. From there, the classroom teacher, reading specialist, paraprofessionals, and interventionists are able to target the varying needs of students based on the results of the assessment. The key to using these data, however, may not be as straightforward as one would think.

Through ongoing analysis and dialogue between teacher and literacy facilitator, the results of the assessments can prove to be an invaluable teaching tool. Keep in mind that these assessments are not written arbitrarily. Great lengths go into determining the type of questions asked and the depth at which knowledge is assessed; equally important, the incorrect student answers are scrutinized in an effort to understand how the student is thinking. These misconceptions can allow the teacher to get to the heart of her students' understanding.

Included in figure 5.1 is an example of a second-grade question and its misconception. The assessment tests word identification skills. As noted, the misconception sheds light into how that child may have misconstrued her thinking. Building misconceptions into the assessment process ensures that every response a student provides offers valuable information about the student's understanding.

Answers *a*, *b*, and *d* demonstrate the varying level of misunderstanding the child may have with respect to initial, medial, and final sounds in words.

Let us take a look at a fourth-grade probe that is assessing making inferences about problem, solution, conflict, and cause/effect (see table 5.2). We should mention that as part of the probe, the student has to first read a passage and then answer the questions.

Question

4. Which word has the same final sound as the last sound in the picture above?
   A. ham
   B. 1ock
   C. tan
   D. pit

Misconceptions

Question number 4	
Question: Which word has the same final sound as the last sound in the picture above?	
Answers	Misconceptions (or correct answer)
a. ham	Similar looking letter
b. lock	Unreasonable
c. tan	Correct answer
d. pit	Same initial sound/letter

Figure 5.1.   Second Grade CFA Question and Misconception

Based on the child's misconception selected, this child's pathway of thinking becomes more apparent. A teacher can better determine if her teaching of this particular standard was effective and for those students who fell short, where their misunderstanding exists.

Teachers find it helpful when the literacy facilitator compiles the data into a visual display, such as a bar graph. The data are given to the classroom

Table 5.2. Fourth Grade CFA Question and Misconception

Question
1. **What caused Sam to pretend he was sick?**
a. Sam didn't like his algebra teacher.
b. He didn't like what they were serving at lunch.
c. Sam had not studied for the test.

Misconceptions

Question number 1 Question: What caused Sam to pretend he was sick?	
Answers	Misconceptions
a. Sam didn't like his algebra teacher.	Inference with no evidence to support it.
b. He didn't like what they were serving at lunch.	Unreasonable
c. Sam had not studied for the test.	Correct answer

teacher in a timely fashion. As seen in the figure 5.2 the graph is a quick snapshot of the percentage of students who grasped the skill in the class and furthermore, how they compared to the other students in that school's grade level (see figure 5.3). At this point, the literacy facilitator guides the classroom teacher into effective management practices. Together, they look at the class as a whole and examine the percentage of students who had difficulty with the various questions. Based on the numbers, they will determine if any incorrect answers are due to instructional or curricular shortcomings.

A large percentage of inaccurate responses for the same question might indicate one of two things: the test question was confusing or the curriculum did not sufficiently address the skill needed for a correct response. If the final determination is that there is a hole in the program, focus lessons can be generated and put into place in a timely manner. If a smaller percentage of students respond incorrectly, it will be assumed that the program's components are adequate, but the students did not master the concept. Those students are "retaught" the skill until they understand and demonstrate it with success.

Looking at the class results in Ms. Smith's class, it is obvious that a high percentage of students understand and can demonstrate their knowledge of some decoding strategies but fall short on others. Consonant and vowel recognition skills proved strong in addition to initial and final sounds, but

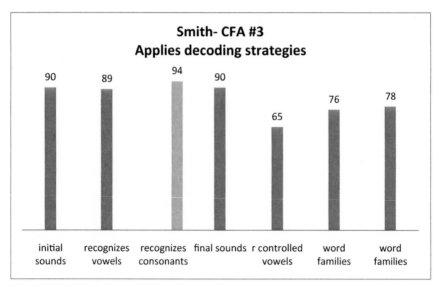

Figure 5.2.   One Second Grade Class's CFA Results

students are still weak in the areas of word families and *r-controlled* vowel patterns. Indeed, this is only one snapshot of a second-grade class. One test is not foolproof. Countless variables can play into the assessment results but this quick, seven-item probe opens the door for:

- Continued needs of the students;
- Targeted intervention in guided reading groups as well as with interventionists;
- Professional development needs;
- Program evaluation; and
- Collegial conversation within a school and district-wide.

Periodically, teachers should be given the opportunity to meet as a grade level to discuss results of the assessments and student learning on a more global scale. At this point, program evaluation takes shape. If consistencies begin to appear among all children in the district at that grade level, one of two problems become evident:1) PD must take place immediately across the district in order to guide teachers in the teaching of that skill or 2) flaws exist in the program's curriculum.

There is also a chance that both factors are playing into the problem. If this is the case, the skill in question must be recorded and the issue brought back to the design team for reevaluation and problem solving. It is the duty

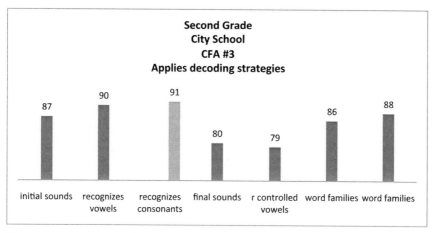

Figure 5.3. Percentage of Correct Answers within the Second Grade Class

of the design team to address all program needs and amend the curriculum as they see fit.

A literacy program created by teachers is constantly evolving to meet the changing needs of both students and teachers. An airtight accountability system, such as the one described here, guarantees to stakeholders that instruction is optimally meeting needs of the diverse student populations. Through this practice, the intricacies of student learning and how it relates to the overall curriculum are at the core of the teachers' professional development.

Elmore (2002) asserts, "if you don't know what kinds of knowledge and skill are required to improve student learning, if you can't recognize different levels of expertise in that core knowledge, and if you don't have a working theory for how to build greater expertise in teaching practice, then it's unlikely that more resources spent on professional development will make any difference to student learning" (p. 19). Reforming instruction by way of a teacher-created reading program ensures that teachers and students work smarter, not harder. Administrators are less likely to expend resources searching for materials (a.k.a. a magic bullet) to ensure student success because the teachers within the district *are* the resources.

VERTICAL ALIGNMENT

Elmore (2003) contests that the common cause of poor-performing schools is getting people to do the *right* work. Few would dispute that most teachers fully invest themselves in their assigned subject matter; however, when the curriculum is unclear, inordinate amounts of time are wasted simply weeding through the standards just to make sense of them. On top of this, overlaps between grade-level expectations can be found in many instances. Some skills are left out of a teacher's curriculum because he may perceive it to be redundant and not appropriate for that grade level, while in other cases, a teacher may teach *everything* outlined for his grade level but never reach the profundity necessary for that skill at that grade level.

When a classroom teacher steps into her classroom, not only should the standards for that grade level/subject area be evident but so too should the levels of complexity. Her starting point and student outcomes must be clearly outlined, eliminating any guesswork. She must be aware of what was taught in the grade before hers and what students will be expected to accomplish at the onset of the next school year.

At that point, she will be better able to begin doing the "right" work. But when a teacher is handed a set of standards, how does she know where to begin? How does she know what the students should come to her classroom knowing and what will be expected of them in the year that follows?

Marzano, Waters, and McNulty (2005) contend that a curriculum must be viable in order for it to be guaranteed. The viability of the curriculum depends upon whether the expectations are realistic given the time restraints within the school day and year. In a home-grown program created by the teachers of the district, one other element comes into play with respect to viability—the needs of the students.

A curriculum cannot be carried out if the instructional delivery of the standards does not take into consideration the learning styles, experiences, and varying needs of the children. Any good educator will tell you that all students engage in learning differently. If that is the case, then the viability of the curriculum must take into account not only the "what" but the "who."

Viability is achieved through the vertical alignment process. Research has shown curriculum alignment to be one of the most compelling strategies educators can implement when ensuring student achievement. When curriculum is aligned within and across the grade levels, the elimination of ambiguous instruction leads to efficient, effective instruction that provides the teacher with student outcome objectives, a scope and sequence, and performance indicators.

Teachers also know what assessments to use and how to use the data to inform their instruction. All stakeholders are guaranteed to some extent that every student in the district is given the same opportunity to learn standards-based content. Teachers from K–12 are aware of subject matter that is emphasized at all grade levels. And through collegial work and conversation, teachers across an entire district understand the academic progression students will encounter as they move between grades. This awareness cannot

Table 5.3. Vertical Alignment of Common Core Standards for Reading Informational Texts

Kindergarten	First	Second	Third	Fourth
Key Ideas and Details in Informational Text				
1. With prompting and support, ask and answer questions about key details in a text.	Ask and answer questions about key details in a text (**independently**).	Ask and answer such questions as **who, what, where, when, why, and how.**	Ask and answer questions to demonstrate understanding of text **referring explicitly to the text as the basis for the answers (citing evidence).**	Refer to the details and examples in a text when explaining what the text says explicitly **and when drawing inferences from the text (citing evidence).**
2. With prompting and support, identify the main topic and retell key details of a text.	Identify the main topic and retell key details of a text (**independently**).	Identify the main topic of a **multi-paragraph text as well as the focus of specific paragraphs within the text.**	**Determine the main idea of a text; recount the key details and explain how they support the main idea.**	Determine the main idea of a text **and explain how it is supported by key details; summarize the text.**
3. With prompting and support, describe the connection between two individuals, events, ideas, or pieces of information in a text.	Describe the connection between two individuals, events, ideas, or pieces of information in a text (**independently**).	Describe the connection between **a series of historical events, scientific ideas or concepts, or steps in technical procedures in a text.**	Describe the relationship between a series of historical events, **scientific ideas or concepts, or steps in technical procedures in a text, using language that pertains to time, sequence, and cause/effect.**	Explain events, procedures, ideas, or concepts in a historical, scientific, or technical text, including what happened and why, **based on specific information in the text.**

occur, however, without constant collaboration and differentiated levels of leadership in the classroom, buildings, and district.

Teachers, literacy facilitators, and administrators must collaborate with people in their schools as well as personnel from each of the other buildings. Through this process, they clarify the essential skills or power standards that must be taught in each grade level and to what extent students are expected to demonstrate mastery. There are even times when a group of teachers will add more substance to a standard to be assured that they are ready for a deeper level of complexity in the years ahead of them.

In table 5.3, you will notice that the common core standards for reading informational text were vertically aligned between grades K–4. The bold print indicates that this skill is introduced for the first time at that grade level. From there, teachers on the design team can unpack the standard by putting it in kid-friendly terms and write a series of focus lessons to guide the teacher in his teaching of the standard with specificity. The skills for that topic that are not in bold are still reviewed and used as a foundation for the newly introduced skill.

For example, identifying the main idea and retelling key details is a skill introduced with support in kindergarten. In first grade, the same skill is taught but because the students were introduced to it in kindergarten, they can now practice the skill independently and the teacher can add another layer of complexity to that skill. At the second-grade level, the students are expected to implement the skill with a higher level of complexity as they engage in longer text. They are taught how to focus on specific information in paragraphs.

By third grade, the students are expected to connect key details to the main idea of the text and explain their relevance. And by fourth grade, the students are responsible for the foundational skill in addition to summarizing the text.

Continuing up through the eighth grade, the students are guaranteed learning this strategy without redundancy. Having the standards aligned vertically also provides the consistency of a common language for both teachers and students. If in kindergarten, the children become familiar with terms such as "summarize" or "key details"; by the time they enter high school, all students are speaking the same language of literacy. This work eliminates unnecessary overlaps and ensures all stakeholders that grade-level skills are taught with continuity and rigor.

SUMMARY

Typically, when a school district makes the commitment to spend money on a prepackaged core literacy program, the majority of its money is spent on the actual materials; it often receives comprehensive kits that include teacher's manuals, workbooks, anthologies, etc. The publisher sends professional developers to the school to "train" the staff in how to use the program, but once the school year is underway, the professional development tends to wane unless the district pays to have other consultants visit the building/district. In a home-grown program, the majority of the money is immediately invested in the knowledge of the practitioners and supplemented with the requisite materials. Furthermore, the list of desired materials evolves as the program blossoms and the teachers' knowledge base develops. Money spent on the time it takes to provide teachers with professional development that is based on the needs of their students is money well spent. By knowing how to use authentic, relevant data, teachers are better able to respond to their students immediately and with urgency, utilizing the strategies that make the most sense, as opposed to waiting for a workshop to come to their city or for a consultant to be available. Purposeful professional development as the foundation of a literacy program ensures the quality teaching that is the heart of reforming literacy instruction.

Chapter Six

Equal Education for All

SNAPSHOT #6

When asked how the district's home-grown literacy program has impacted his instruction, fourth grade teacher David Goldsmith explained, "It has stopped me from lying." Asked to explain, he went on to share that prior to the implementation of the district's home-grown program, the way in which he taught reading was authentic, using real texts and based on proven research. There were no scripts because what he taught was designed specifically for his students. He had felt for many years that when he shut the door to his classroom and taught reading with his materials and in a manner that suited his children as opposed to how the purchased core program demanded, he was somehow "breaking the rules."

Unbeknownst to him, others all over the school and district, for that matter, were doing the same thing. "Now I don't have to lie. It's like coming clean, really. I can actually talk about this (reading instruction) and we are now talking about this as a district. I feel comfortable as a teacher with my beliefs actually having a place where people aren't rolling their eyes at the 'hippie kid' who wants his students to read real books."

He went on to talk about the impact of having shared experiences across the district and how much easier it will be to teach his incoming students now, confident that they will come to him with common, authentic experiences on which he can build. These experiences are far beyond what the teacher's manual or basal someone else wrote says his students *should* learn regardless of their backgrounds, needs, or learning styles.

"I detest basals to such a degree that if we went back to one, I would have to lie again. Knowing that we have a program that is focused on the needs of our students and actually creates the teacher as professional-model, I think, enriches all of our lives." He elaborates that although standards drive the lessons, the delivery of instruction is dynamic. Some instruction such as cursive or chemistry requires one set way in order to reach an objective; reading does not. "Teaching cursive is teaching cursive but reading is like. . . . If I had to teach breathing, I wouldn't want to do it with a basal."

BUT I WANT TO BE WITH THE "COOL" KIDS

Anyone who has ever learned a new sport as an adult can attest to the cruelty of it all. Let's take skiing as an example. For children learning to ski, there is no regard for the embarrassment that comes with falling down on a flat surface, getting tangled up in the lift, or even the fact that the only way down a trail is by way of the dreaded, thigh-burning snowplow or, as a five-year-old calls it, the "pizza" stance.

As rational adults, we tend to go through the proper channels of learning. Hire an instructor, wear the proper protection, and have copious amounts of pain reliever on stand-by. We purchase or rent equipment that is appropriate to our level of expertise (in most cases, very short skis) even though we really want to step into the bindings of the skis the "cool kids" are using.

Alas, we plod along practicing on the novice trail, but only so many exercises with the assistance of the instructor on the flatter terrain will improve our ability to ski. Eventually, we will have to take off on our own, experience more difficult slopes, and independently implement the skills that our instructor taught us. We will fall and become embarrassed, especially when this happens under the ascending chairlift; but without this process we will not learn.

We cannot stay on the bunny slope for the entire ski season if we want to someday ski the black diamond–rated trails. This does not mean that we cannot go back time and time again and take another lesson, but if we were to continue only practicing the snowplow stance, we would never develop a love and passion for skiing. If we never had the opportunity to get off the bunny slope and ride the chairlift to the top where most of the other skiers ski and the views are spectacular, our attitude toward skiing would be quite negative—we would never ski unless we absolutely had to. This is how we must look at struggling readers.

In Kucer's book *What Research Really Says about Teaching and Learning to Read* (2008), Michael Shaw discusses the dichotomy between the "Cycle of Success" and the "Cycle of Failure." In the cycle of failure, a struggling reader who is expected to engage in reading activities that are not differentiated begins to feel defeated and overwhelmed with the process, eventually giving in to that defeat. This child sees herself as not fitting in with the rest of the children in the class and shuts off to any further instruction. The problem perpetuates itself.

Conversely, in a classroom where the teacher is aware of all children's strengths and weaknesses, the instruction is catered to each child within the whole-class instruction, enrichment, or intervention. He attends to their level and empowers all students. It is an expectation in his classroom that every child will be a successful reader and writer; he is committed to recognizing ALL students for their successes.

In this scenario, children are surrounded by books and materials that are specifically at their level. They receive targeted interventions if necessary in addition to guaranteed time with their teacher in guided reading groups or individual reading conferences. If an outsider were to set foot in this classroom, it would be difficult to determine which students are below grade level.

Based on his research, Shaw (in Kucer, 2008, p.203) goes on to say "we have learned that instruction for readers who struggle should not be a different type of instruction than that provided for all students, but we need to be more systematic and explicit through multiple demonstrations; and we need to provide more intense opportunities for guided and independent practice to reinforce skills and strategies."

To refer back to the skiing metaphor, beginning skiers do not need different equipment when learning; they simply need equipment that meets their needs—shorter skis, no ski poles, plenty of Ibuprofen, and so on. Every time they feel confident enough to move to a higher slope, they are encouraged to do so. It is important to keep in mind that even the most advanced skiers regularly utilize a basic set of fundamental strategies that they were taught early on. Without them, they would not successfully complete the trail. Skiers build on the fundamentals as they advance.

Comprehensive literacy instruction reform includes all aspects of what every child will need in order to understand and contribute to the written and spoken word in the outside world, regardless of ability. Figure 6.1 illustrates those essential components of reading instruction: phonological/phonemics awareness, phonics, decoding, comprehension, fluency, and vocabulary instruction; however, it also encompasses word study/spelling, intervention needs, and content area literacy.

In this chapter we will focus on the impact word study and vocabulary instruction can have on students, particularly those who struggle in literacy. We will also examine the effects collaborative approaches to intervention can have on struggling readers and writers.

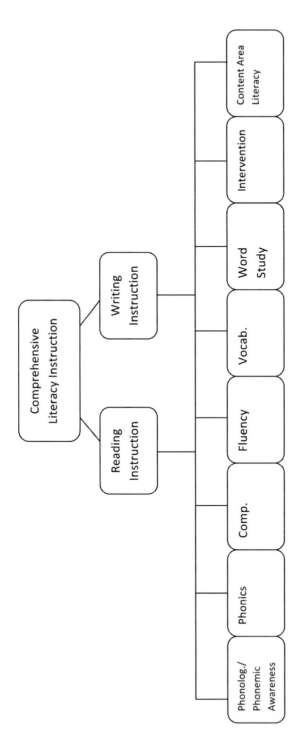

Figure 6.1. The Framework for Comprehensive Literacy Instruction within a Home-Grown Program

PARALLELED INSTRUCTION

In a teacher-created program, the overall delivery of instruction is designed so that the most advanced student practices the same skill alongside the less accomplished. This way, both types of students come to understand the purpose for reading within their own levels of text. Classroom teachers and interventionists are mindful of the strategies a less accomplished reader must learn in order to excel. In their intervention groups, they provide ample time to teach the skills that need improving as well as how to implement them in authentic text. If the goal of reading instruction is to move children toward an understanding and appreciation for the written word, it should not matter if a child is reading at a level *C* or level *T*.

All developing readers must be given the opportunity and resources to become reflective readers who see reading as a purposeful activity. For both the accomplished and the struggling reader, teachers must guide them to set purposes for reading, so they know *why* they are reading (Shaw in Kucer, 2008). It is the responsibility of the classroom teacher and interventionist to perpetuate the cycle of success.

There is no denying that we read for a plethora of reasons—to get through day-to-day activities, excel in our jobs, enhance our lives, and so on. Whether it is through fiction or informational text, accomplished readers eventually master strategies that help them make sense of what they are reading. Due to a wealth of research on learning to read, we now know that reading comprehension is more than just remembering the words on the page; in fact, the process of comprehension involves a multitude of strategies at play at various times.

Predicting, summarizing, synthesizing, and making connections while reading are just a few of the strategies a reader must learn in order to be able to engage in meaningful conversations around text or if nothing else, to "prove" they truly understood what they read. In order to engage in thoughtful literacy (Allington 2006), students must be taught these strategies and how to implement them as they travel through texts. This includes and may even be more crucial for the below grade-level readers who become used to learning how to decode but not how to think about what they are reading.

If we examine the types of questions that students are responsible for answering on an informal reading inventory such as the DRA (Beaver 2004) or Benchmark Assessment (Fountas & Pinnell 2008), it is clear that students are expected to think *within, beyond,* and *about* the text while reading. The questions asked of students on those assessments determine the depth of thinking that occurs at the various reading levels. They assume that students at all levels are learning and practicing a set of foundational reading strategies such as self-monitoring, connecting text content to situations in real life or other texts, confirming or disconfirming predictions, identifying turning points in the story, and so on, with the expectation that these strategies will become more complex as the student moves up in levels.

If the struggling reader is ever going to move beyond the low-level texts, he must be provided with the tools necessary to be ready to think at more complex levels in addition to the decoding strategies typically taught during intervention. Changing the structure of intervention to the point where thinking strategies hold the same weight as decoding strategies is a key component in reforming the way all students receive reading instruction, whether in the classroom or resource room.

Let us illustrate the way in which a home-grown reading program responds to the needs of a struggling student. Jimmy is a student in Mrs. Hall's second-grade class. He has been considered below grade level in reading since first grade and began receiving intervention services about midway through that year. He was tested for a variety of learning impairments but nothing substantial surfaced. Now in second grade, he continues to see the reading specialist four times a week for half-hour intervention blocks. Jimmy struggles primarily with decoding which of course impacts his comprehension and fluency.

During his intervention block, the reading specialist spends approximately ten minutes focusing on word work (e.g., various vowel sounds, digraphs, syllables, etc.). She provides him with decoding strategies such as tapping out sounds, using context clues, and so on. For the next ten to fifteen minutes, Jimmy is engaged in reading an instructional-level text along with other members in this 2–3 person group. The children discuss the topic of the day's focus lesson. It may be on how to sequence story parts or how to infer a character's feelings.

Regardless of the level of text, the students in Jimmy's group are always shown how the skills their teacher demonstrated in the focus lesson fit into the broader picture when reading their instructional-level texts. For the last five to ten minutes with the reading specialist, Jimmy will engage in a writing activity that corresponds to the book he is reading and the skill he is practicing. When Jimmy returns to his classroom, there is approximately twenty minutes left in the readers' workshop.

Since Jimmy enjoys reading on his own and is capable of sustaining independent reading without any problems, he may practice his newly learned skills in a book that he has chosen from his book box. The books in his box are a mixture of mostly independent-level texts chosen with guidance from his teacher. Throughout the week, Mrs. Hall will check in with Jimmy during an individual reading conference in order to reinforce and check on how he is implementing reading strategies.

Depending on the student and classroom teacher, students like Jimmy may get a combination of time with an interventionist and time with the classroom teacher in a guided reading group. They will also have time to read independently each day. At all times students are engaged in authentic texts and practicing strategies that every developing reader needs.

Each student in the classroom has the same task to complete during readers' workshop. For example, if the focus lesson was on an author's message, every student will be responsible at the "wrap-up" of the readers' workshop to show evidence of that practiced skill. Even if Jimmy was engaged in a level *D* text, he is just as responsible as his classmate who is reading a level *O* text for discussing the intended message of the text.

Regardless of the child's needs, IEP (Individualized Education Program) parameters, personnel boundaries, or schedule restraints, in a home-grown literacy program, all children remain in the classroom at the onset and conclusion of the readers'/writers' workshop. They take part in the focus lesson with their peers and come back to the room for the wrap-up and share at the conclusion of the workshop. They are always encouraged to demonstrate their discoveries and learning. This ensures that each student, no matter the level of learning, is exposed to, encouraged to, and held accountable to grade-level expectations.

Since collaboration is a cornerstone of a home-grown program, it is expected that special educators, tutors, and any other support staff be a regular part of their child's classroom. It is crucial that classroom instruction and targeted intervention be delivered as seamlessly as possible.

STUDENT AND TEACHER INTERVENTIONS

We don't know what we don't know—a teacher can only teach what she knows to be best practice. If a teacher thinks that her instruction is effective and no one is telling her otherwise it is unlikely that her less than effective practices will ever improve. If the "pick and choose" professional development model prevalent in most schools across the country remains as is, this learned helplessness will perpetuate with discouraging outcomes. The teacher will only choose what appears interesting to her, not necessarily what she really needs.

But if all classroom teachers are expected to look introspectively at their teaching and their students' progress, knowing that they will be provided with the same knowledge and expertise a special educator or reading specialist possesses, there is hope for change. Instead of "bypassing" (Allington, 2006) the problem, ineffective classroom teaching must be looked at as the root of the problem and attended to immediately through worthwhile professional development that targets the needs of the teachers.

There will always be students who benefit from one-on-one or small group interventions provided by a teacher specializing in that area of instruction, but if more classroom teachers are trained in intensive methods that may thwart future reading difficulties children may encounter, it is our hope that the numbers of students in need of special services will begin to diminish. Intervention programs delivered by "specialists" should not be so heavily relied on as they currently are in many schools.

In one school that was implementing their home-grown literacy program, the first grade teachers were dissatisfied with the numbers of students who were running into decoding obstacles at various points in the school year. They were given time to analyze data and collaborate with one another on various teaching strategies. Curious as to how a reading specialist would tackle such issues, they sought the guidance of the literacy facilitator.

This collaboration resulted in designated time each week for the literacy facilitator to come into their classrooms and model various decoding strategies for their whole class. All students were shown how to "tap out" sounds in words as part of a systematic, phonics-based approach to teaching word study. The literacy facilitator guided the first-grade teachers in developing differentiated materials that matched the phonics principles in the program's word study component for encoding and decoding. She also made them aware of the "rules" prevalent in spelling, such as the varying types of syllables.

This intervention resulted in coordinated instruction and confident, knowledgeable word study teachers within the entire first grade. The approach proved beneficial for the support staff as well. Since all students were learning the same strategies, those who visited the reading specialist and special education staff for intervention came knowing a very effective strategy, allowing teachers to spend their time further strengthening their students' decoding or focusing on other areas of difficulty.

Best of all, children who were leaving the classroom for extra support began to see themselves as less "different" than their first-grade peers because they were all practicing the same strategies at varying degrees; all students, at times, needed to "tap out" words. It became a common practice.

In this case, the teachers became the experts because they were on the receiving end of the intervention. Due to immediate, job-embedded professional development, the first-grade teachers were given the tools they needed for a series of weeks in order to blend their instruction with that of the reading specialists and special educators. They maximized their instructional time with their students, ultimately lifting some of the burden off special services in the first grade. Looking to be responsive educators, these professionals sought and received the resources that were necessary to be proactive rather than reactive.

This model is not exclusive to the primary grades. Its replication is plausible at the intermediate level to include training for classroom teachers who want to inform their teaching or to be ready and armed with the strategies necessary to stave off any possible obstacles their older, struggling readers may encounter. This may include comprehension strategies, vocabulary practice, or strategies to better teach students to connect reading and writing by responding to literature.

INTERMEDIATE INTERVENTIONS—INCLUDING LITERACY IN THE CONTENT AREAS

For many years, great emphasis has been placed on pushing students to learn the fundamental strategies of good reading in the early grades, typically K–3, and there is a plethora of research to support this thinking. In terms of intervention, schools tend to load their primary grades with countless hours of research–based intervention techniques and programs, hoping to avoid seeing any student leave third grade below grade level in reading. The fear is if a child enters fourth grade with any reading difficulties, it becomes much more difficult to "remediate" the student and the chances are high that her difficulties will compound throughout the years. This is likely to occur if the child is left to her own devices upon entering fourth grade; however, recent research shows this to be untrue if these students' needs are recognized and addressed.

In Richard Allington's book, *What Really Matters to Struggling Readers: Designing Research-Based Programs* (2006), he rejects this grim view by referring to studies purporting that older readers are able to make significant gains if they have access to targeted, rigorous instruction that is delivered by an expert in reading instruction (Davidson & Koppenhaver; Krashen, Morris, Ervin; and Conrad Showers, Joyce, Scanlon, & Schnaubelt, in Allington 2006). Schools are realizing the need to provide equal amounts of intervention at the intermediate grades, but still, the change is slow.

This shift in attitude requires yet another "reculturation" (Hargreaves and Fullan 1998) if reform is to happen. Schools need to re-evaluate, reorganize, and restructure the way they deliver reading support to their students. It would be negligent to ignore the preponderance of evidence suggesting the need for early reading intervention, but through a teacher-designed program, a framework can be developed that includes in-class and out-of-class support for students who struggle in the grades beyond third grade.

Classroom teachers design focus lessons that can be practiced by all students regardless of their reading level, as illustrated in the Jimmy scenario. For example, a fourth grader reading a level *J* book can practice the skill of noticing character motives just as his peer reading a level *U* book. Because the schedule is carefully thought out to include uninterrupted blocks of literacy time, all interventionists are available during the fourth-grade readers' workshop time to work with struggling readers, either in their classroom or in a resource room/literacy lab environment.

Reading skills instruction cannot end as students enter their intermediate years if they are expected to develop into competent, thoughtful readers (Allington, 2006). Struggling readers must be assured support as text complexities increase, and content-area classes place a greater emphasis on reading. In a home-grown literacy program, equal time is given to intermediate students because the schedule, curriculum framework, and materials allow for it.

THE VALUE OF INFORMATIONAL TEXTS

One key factor in a teacher-created literacy program that we believe is integral to students' success in the later years is the emphasis on informational texts at the primary grades as well as intermediate. Allington (2006) calls for reading instruction in the early grades to include "how" to read informational texts in order to prepare students for what's to come in the intermediate grades.

This includes using a variety of instructionally appropriate texts that share the same features of the more complex content-based books or even traditional textbooks that one might encounter in middle school or even high school. Instructing students early on how to approach an informational text with the strategies necessary to extrapolate relevant information will provide more room for content area learning since the burden of "figuring out" the text has been lifted.

Duke's (in Allington, 2006) research found primary-grade students reading informational texts only 3.6 minutes per day, not even scraping the surface of their capabilities. Furthermore, she contends that the research outlines four guiding principles for increasing student achievement with respect to informational texts:

- Increase student access to a variety of informational texts.
- Increase the time students spend working with informational texts.
- Teach specific comprehension strategies for reading informational texts.
- Provide opportunities for students to use informational texts authentically (Duke in Allington 2006).

Based on first-grade reading and writing standards, one set of teachers designed an informational text unit that included lessons on:

- Informational text features (table of contents, index, diagrams, etc.)
- Approach to reading fiction versus nonfiction texts
- Accumulating a variety of information on the same topic
- Using texts to answer questions about a topic
- Putting newly learned information into their own words
- Combining schemata with new information to formulate inferences

As you can see, these higher order thinking skills are not left to the inter-mediate grades. Within the informational text unit, these teachers are laying the groundwork for what is to come in the subsequent years. First-grade students spend upwards of three months focusing on learning nonfiction reading strategies. They also practice these strategies as writers since their writing units coincide with reading.

Placing a heavy emphasis on informational text should not stop at the classroom door. In fact, if instructional reform is to occur systemically, the use of informational text must be commonplace within all intervention programs as well. Tutors, special educators, and reading specialists must also incorporate informational text in day-to-day reading instruction in order to provide struggling readers with the skills necessary to learn content material alongside their peers. That being said, it is imperative that all educators be cognizant of the background knowledge each student brings to the informational text as he reads. This is particularly crucial in those classrooms that include children from a variety of socioeconomic backgrounds. More time may be needed to build schemata on a topic before students engage in text or writing about text. Even at the earliest grades, students may need additional instruction on how activating their background knowledge on a specific topic will enhance their decoding and comprehension while reading. In schools where children have less opportunity to learn about the world around them, literacy instruction that includes informational text is of the utmost importance.

VOCABULARY AND DIFFERENTIATED WORD STUDY

Vocabulary Instruction

A wave of research has surfaced heralding the significance of vocabulary instruction, especially in classrooms of children from low socioeconomic backgrounds. At the forefront of this research are Beck, McKeown, and Kucan who in their book, *Bringing Words to Life: Robust Vocabulary*

Instruction (2002), contend that direct, robust vocabulary instruction directly affects reading comprehension. This means students are taught and expected to use words that are rich, powerful, and go beyond the more "common" words of everyday language.

Through vocabulary instruction, children as early as kindergarten should be exposed to words that will have profound effects on their speaking, listening, reading, and writing. The authors refer to Smith's study (in Beck, McKeown, and Kucan, 2002) that shows that high school students graduating at the top of their class knew about four times as many words as their lower performing classmates. And, the higher achieving third graders he studied had vocabularies that were equal to the lowest performing twelfth graders.

A perfect storm must occur in order for all students to attain a level of vocabulary that is commensurate with high achievement. The child's schemata must be rich; he must read enough to be exposed to wide-ranging vocabulary, and he must be immersed in an environment that encourages the use of newly acquired vocabulary. Those students who are below grade level readers and/or come from homes without language-rich environments are already at a disadvantage. Direct vocabulary instruction at school is a necessary component that a quality literacy program cannot live without.

Although the evidence is becoming more plentiful, few prepackaged, core programs include an ample amount of vocabulary instruction to bring all children up to a leveled playing field regardless of home situations. Few prepackaged core programs provide students from homes with limited language the quality of words a student will need in order to keep up with her peers in the middle- and high-school years. Included in the process of reforming literacy instruction is designated time set aside to teach higher level vocabulary.

Direct instruction of vocabulary is crucial if content area reading instruction is to be effective, since part of vocabulary instruction is the building or activation of a child's schemata. The child learns or is reminded of a concept through teacher-led classroom discussion, who perhaps uses pictures to illustrate the idea, and then gives the word to represent that idea. Children are expected to identify that word if they see it in their texts and they are expected to use the word in context, but spelling it is not required. When the word is encountered down the road, there is little chance that it will hinder the child's reading process.

When discussing the struggles of older readers and why they tend to encounter countless obstacles when reading, Allington (2006) refers to Ivey and Baker's (2004) work that explains that when a student comes across a word that is unknown, particularly in content area texts where the vocabulary tends to be big and new, the child does not possess the background knowledge necessary to tackle the word and move on.

In a home-grown literacy program, teachers are teaching words that are specific to the needs of their students, keeping in mind their schemata and life experiences. Students are even encouraged to use their newly learned words in their writing (although precise spelling is not crucial), ensuring that the learning is solidified. This includes the words students will need to be familiar with in all content areas including math.

Word Study Instruction

Furthermore, teachers instruct children on Greek and Latin roots, prefixes, and suffixes during their word study so that even within vocabulary instruction, the student can make some sense of "how" the words work—students are exposed to the interconnectedness of vocabulary and word study. As early as first grade, students at all learning levels begin to see the connections involved in spelling. They begin to use analytical approaches to decoding: for example, understanding how the learning of one word family can help with decoding a multitude of other words. Along with learning short and long vowel patterns, they begin to see how prefixes like *un-, re-, and dis-* can change the definition of a word and when *–ing* or *–ed* are added to the end of a word, depending on the part of speech or tense change. Spelling is transformed into word study.

When the teachers are the architects of the program, all students' encoding abilities are taken into account. Students are not all given the same list on Monday and expected to memorize for a spelling test on Friday. Instead, every student in the class is given a list of words on a par with their level of encoding that requires them to practice the principle of the week.

How to provide the words to students is left up to the teacher so students are assured that the words they are responsible for will be appropriate to their ability. For instance, if a second-grade class's principle of the week is the diphthong spelled *oi,* or *oy*, all students will practice this pattern, from the special education student up to the child who is receiving enrichment. The word *joy* may be on one child's list, while the words *enjoy, toil,* or *foist* may be on others'.

A great emphasis on words that have definitional value is considered when creating word lists. In other words, just because the word may be somewhat easy for a child to spell does not mean that he knows the meaning of the word. As illustrated in the word *foist,* an advanced second-grade speller could spell that word without issue, but knowing what the word means or how to use it properly in a sentence is an important component of a comprehensive, differentiated word study program that takes vocabulary knowledge into account.

SUMMARY

The goal of any district interested in reforming literacy instruction should include ALL students. This cannot happen without every teacher, specialist, interventionist, support staff, and administration working together. In present-day public schools, children are grouped according to their age. Whether this is right or wrong, it is the system we use.

It does not take long for an educator to realize that, although this system may not work effectively, we must work within its boundaries. In a curriculum that responds to the needs of the students, the idea of "where they are supposed to be" takes a back seat. Instead, the instruction presented to that child takes into account who the student is as a person, where he has come from, and where he has the potential to go. In addition, teachers implementing the program are listened to, with respect to their needs, so that they can develop as professionals who utilize effective teaching strategies that respond to the diverse needs of their students each year.

No one involved in any type of instructional reform will claim that this is an easy process, but when all of the pieces of a comprehensive literacy program come together, the objectives are clear and the road to reach them is with few obstacles. The beauty of a program that evolves out of the minds of teachers is the ability to add to it or take away from it if necessary. In this day and age, it is doubtful that much is ever eliminated from a literacy curriculum; in fact, for most teachers, too much is piled on each year.

Their students' needs get more complicated and parents expect more than what some teachers feel they can offer. But if all students are to be given the opportunity to develop into literate members of society, contributing to the betterment of the world, it only makes sense that they are given the tools that each one requires, in a manner that matches who they are as learners. Everyone deserves the opportunity to make it to the top of the mountain and to enjoy the thrill of the ride down.

Chapter Seven

Oh Yeah? Prove It!

SNAPSHOT #7

The school district under focus took a distinct leap of faith in their teachers when they allowed them to virtually throw away their formulaic curriculum guides in favor of creating their own kindergarten through eighth grade teacher-created literacy program. In the midst of the standards era, state and national assessments, AYP and Schools In Need of Improvement Reports, this administration demonstrated Herculean faith in their teachers' professional knowledge, skills, and drive. They had no reason to believe that this teacher-written curriculum would be any more effective than the published curricula, with their well-respected authors and their mountains of research briefs; in fact, they had many reasons to believe that it would be less effective.

The achievement of this coordinated curriculum was due to a ripe mixture of political, practical, and professional savvy, which started two years earlier. The district's curriculum coordinator wrote in her "Executive Summary" to the school board that this curriculum endeavor was born in response to teacher input that a commercially published literacy program "would not meet the diverse needs of all students and might marginalize teachers by not allowing them autonomy to make decisions about how best to teach reading to their students" (Briggs-Badger 2009, p. 1).

The "Executive Summary" listed the foundational components as the cornerstone of the program:

- Shared beliefs about learning and literacy
- Clearly articulated standards and goals for reading instruction
- Underlying principles of the reading process and the development of a reader

- Essential components of effective reading instruction
- Necessary infrastructure for supporting literacy
- A culture of collegiality, collaboration and support for our classroom teachers, special educators, reading specialists and literacy facilitators (Briggs-Badger 2009)

While anecdotal responses were affirming of the program itself and the enthusiasm of the students and teachers was extremely positive, it became necessary to support those qualitative reactions with numbers. A formal program evaluation was enacted to give all stakeholders the opportunity to systematically gather data, which enabled administration and staff to monitor progress toward program goals, to learn from mistakes, and to make modifications as needed to judge the success of the program in achieving its short-term and long-term outcomes.

Through systematic evaluation, this district was able to track changes in student literacy achievement as well as teacher attitudes and competencies resulting from the implementation of this teacher-created literacy program.

The formal program evaluation investigated the following anticipated outcomes:

- To monitor progress toward the program's goals.
- To determine whether program components are producing the desired progress on outcomes.
- To permit comparisons among groups, particularly among populations with high risk factors (English for Speakers of Other Languages (ESOL), Low Socioeconomic Status (SES), Special Education students).
- To justify the need for further funding and support from the school board, administration and curriculum planning committee.
- To pinpoint opportunities for continuous quality improvement.
- To ensure that effective components of the program are maintained and strengthened.

As in the snapshot above, a program evaluation can be a useful tool for a school district to evaluate curriculum. Sound data on the impact of any teacher-created program is crucial in order for the district to move forward with confidence that they are providing the most effective literacy instruction for all students involved. In addition to verifying that students are progressing, a formal evaluation can also provide critical information about components that may not be working at peak performance so individual constructs can be tweaked.

This chapter will be dedicated to constructing a manageable evaluation of the teacher-created literacy program in order to inform the users and the public about its efficacy. We will discuss evaluation questions, identify key stakeholders, review the design of data collection, and explore ways to disseminate the information discovered.

According to Stufflebeam and Shinkfield (2007), leading scholars in program evaluation, the main uses for an evaluation are for "improvement, accountability, dissemination, and enlightenment" (p. 22). Historically, when implementing innovations, school personnel are apt to "throw the baby out with the bath water" and a program evaluation will guard against that temptation.

A program evaluation does not need to be costly or time consuming and can be included as an element of school-wide or district-wide reflective professional development. Additionally, individual teachers or professional learning communities may consider conducting action research on the literacy curriculum as part of their yearly goals.

Due to accountability trends in education, documentation and analysis of student achievement is already a common practice in schools. The format of a program evaluation will provide some consistency and formality to the process; keep in mind that any proposed evaluation would need to include both a formative and a summative component.

Formative data will give users information that can lead to better and more effective practices with the intention of strengthening the entire literacy program. The formative component will consist of classroom observations, assessment data, surveys and questionnaires, and individual and focus group interviews with district staff, students, and parents.

Summative data will be useful in determining the effectiveness of the program's goal of raising student achievement for all students, in particular the success of ESOL, low SES and Special Education students. It will provide an analysis and comparison of test score data across a historical and current perspective of school and district results on measures of standardized assessment.

Evaluation Questions to Guide the Evaluation

Prior to beginning a program evaluation, it is necessary to revisit the original goals of a teacher-created curriculum. Revisiting the goals will allow those involved in the evaluation to format interview and focus group questions that align with the data you want to collect. It is necessary to restate original goals into questions as well as add some additional questions. Table 7.1 provides a sample.

Table 7.1.   Teacher-Created Program Goals and Evaluation Questions

Major Program Goals	Questions to Guide the Evaluation
1. Align literacy instruction across the schools in the district	Has the home-grown program led to alignment of classroom materials and instructional practices across the schools involved?
2. Raise student achievement in literacy across the student population, including ESOL, Low SES and Special Education students	Is there an effect on student achievement scores on measures of standardized assessments as a result of the literacy curriculum?
	What impact, if any, does the new curriculum have on the achievement of previously underperforming subgroups in literacy (ex. ESOL, Low SES and Special Education students)?
3. Equip all schools and classrooms with access to quality literature and materials	Do all classrooms have access to quality literature and materials?
4. Strive for student personalized instruction	Is there an emphasis on student personalized instruction?
5. Provide intervention for struggling readers	Do we have a system to catch and assist struggling readers early?
	In what ways, if at all, has the home-grown program contributed to the development of professional knowledge of school staff in matters of literacy learning and acquisition?
	In what ways are teachers satisfied/ dissatisfied with the teacher-created literacy program?
6. Establish ongoing, embedded professional development	

Key Stakeholders

After aligning the program goals to the evaluation questions, one of the next steps in a program evaluation of this sort is to identify and engage stakeholders (Stufflebeam and Shinkfield, 2007). Stakeholders are people or organizations that are invested in the program, are interested in the results of the evaluation, and/or have a stake in what will be done with the results of the evaluation. Representing their needs and interests throughout the process is fundamental to good program evaluation. See table 7.2.

Table 7.2. Identifying Key Stakeholders for the Home-Grown Literacy Curriculum

Those involved in using the teacher-created literacy curriculum	*Those served or affected by the literacy curriculum and instruction*	*The primary users of the evaluation results*
Teachers	Students	School Administration:
School Administration:	Parents	Literacy Facilitators
Literacy Facilitators		Federal Projects Director
Curriculum Coordinator		Curriculum Coordinator
Federal Projects Director		Teachers
		School Board
		Curriculum Planning Committee

Key stakeholders for a teacher-created literacy curriculum typically fall into three main groups:

- Those involved in *program operations*
- Those *served or affected* by the program
- Those who are intended *users* of the evaluation findings

Evaluation Design

Phase 1: Formative Evaluation—CIPP Model

Stufflebeam's CIPP model of program evaluation aligns best for guiding evaluative decisions regarding the formative aspects of a teacher-created literacy curriculum. This model is well suited to an evaluation of literacy curriculum because its tenets of "stimulating, aiding and abetting efforts to strengthen and improve" programs corresponds to the goals of a teacher-created program (p. 331). Included in the CIPP model are evaluations of a program's "Context, Inputs, Processes, and Products," all with a focus on improvement, planning and implementation efforts of a program (p. 327).

Two anticipated outcomes of improvement-oriented evaluations, such as the CIPP model, are especially relevant to the evaluation of a new curriculum, namely to "1) foster improvement and accountability through information and assessing program decisions, 2) assist consumers to make wise choices among optional programs and services" (p. 197). Table 7.3 depicts the goals

Table 7.3. Evaluation Focus Questions and Data Source Identified

Evaluation Focus Questions	Data Sources/Methods of Collection
Has the home-grown program led to alignment of classroom materials and instructional practices across the schools involved?	Literacy Facilitators/Document Analysis, Observation, Survey
Is there an effect on student achievement scores on measures of standardized assessments as a result of the literacy curriculum?	Principals and Superintendent/School and District State Assessment Reports
What impact, if any, does the new curriculum have on the achievement of previously underperforming subgroups in literacy (ex. ESOL, Low SES and Special Education students)?	Special Education Teacher, English as Second Language Teacher, Reading Specialist, etc. Document Analysis, School, District and State Assessment
In what ways, if at all, has the program contributed to the development of professional knowledge of school staff in matters of literacy learning and acquisition?	Literacy Facilitators, Principals, Teachers/Surveys, questionnaires, PD Menus, Observations
In what ways are teachers satisfied/dissatisfied with the literacy program?	Teachers/Teacher Satisfaction Survey

of the sample evaluation questions and the method of data collection that addresses each goal.

If teachers are achieving efficacy while teaching, they are more apt to persist through difficult challenges, experiment with different methods, and internally minimize negative emotions. If we believe that the literacy curriculum has the ability to affect teachers' efficacy, we must ask for their feedback and address any concerns. Tables 7.4 and 7.5 are templates for requesting written feedback from users of a home-grown program while below is a protocol for small-group discussions.

Protocol for Small-Group Discussions. *Focus Group Interview Questions for Resource Management Worksheet*

- In what ways do the resources you have for literacy instruction enhance teacher effectiveness? If it is a barrier to program success, please explain.
- How do the resources you have for literacy instruction impact program quality?
- Suggestions for change.

Table 7.4. Teacher Satisfaction Survey

Status of Teacher-Created Literacy Curriculum–Teacher Satisfaction Survey

Grade Level _____   Total Minutes Per Week you are able to devote to:
Readers' Workshop _____
Word Study _____
Writers' Workshop _____
Small Group Instruction _____

Component	Highly Effective	Moderately Effective	Marginally Effective	Not Effective	Comments
Guided Strategy lesson					
Guided Reading Materials					
Teacher-Created Curriculum Binder					
Word Study Binder					
Writer's Workshop Professional Materials					
Literacy Facilitator PD Model					
Workshop Model for Reading Instruction					
Workshop Model for Writing Instruction					
Stable daily schedule for uninterrupted reading block					
Special education integrated with classroom instruction					
Student achievement data regularly reviewed by teacher and literacy facilitator together					
Appropriate professional development coordinated by literacy facilitator					
Program fidelity					
Use of state standards/common core standards for reading achievement					

Table 7.5. Time and Resource Management Teacher Survey and Questionnaire

Adequate Time and Resources Allocated	Highly Effective	Moderately Effective	Minimally Effective
Teacher Professional Development			
Instructional Planning			
Assessment			
Literacy Facilitating (modeling, resource sharing, feedback, planning)			
Uninterrupted block of daily reading			
Additional opportunities daily for supplemental instruction			
Additional opportunities daily for intervention instruction			

Phase 2: Summative Evaluation—Quasi-Experimental Model

If the CIPP model of program evaluation is able to generate data suggesting that the teacher-created curriculum has been implemented with fidelity throughout the school or district, it may be prudent to conduct a quasi-experimental evaluation as a summative addition to the CIPP model. The experimental design approach to evaluation produces data that can potentially be used to make causal claims regarding the effects of the program (Stufflebeam 2007). However, designing a true experiment in school settings is complicated and sometimes unethical as it calls for control groups, random assignment, and the withholding of treatment to certain participants.

Fortunately, there are some steps that can be taken that preserve the integrity of the experiment design in social contexts such as school. One of those options is to use a quasi-experimental design. A quasi-experimental design makes comparisons between nonequivalent groups and does not require random assignment and control groups (Stufflebeam, 2007). A quasi-experimental approach will allow users of the results to potentially make claims attributing any change in student literacy achievement to the literacy program when compared with the literacy achievement of statistically similar schools and districts.

Analyzing the Information

According to Stufflebeam and Shinkfield (2007), information collected in an evaluation provides an "evidentiary basis for answering priority questions" (p. 587). Each source of information gathered for this evaluation should be thoroughly described and analyzed to provide a foundation for justifiable

Table 7.6. Types and Sources of Data for Analysis

Type and Source of Information	Qualitative or Quantitative Data?	Analysis of the Information
Interviews	Qualitative	Thematic analysis of transcripts
Surveys	Quantitative	Descriptive statistics
Questionnaires	Qualitative	Thematic analysis
Observation	Qualitative	Thematic analysis
Document analysis	Quantitative	Descriptive statistics, Analysis of variance

conclusions. The Timeline in table 7.6 documents the types and sources of information that will be collected in synthesizing conclusions.

Phase 3: Disseminating Results

Dissemination is the process of communicating evaluation procedures or lessons learned to relevant audiences in a timely, unbiased, and consistent manner. The goal for dissemination is to achieve full disclosure and impartial reporting. Table 7.7 details a sample plan for disseminating results from the literacy program evaluation.

Table 7.7. Plan for Disseminating Literacy Results

Audiences	How to Share Results
Teachers	Abstract and handout distributed and discussed at monthly staff meeting with question/answer session
School Administration	Abstract and handout distributed and discussed at District Literacy Team meeting . . . possible PowerPoint presentation
District Literacy Team	Abstract and handout distributed and discussed at District Literacy Team meeting
Students	Information presented to students by their classroom and literacy (homeroom) teachers
Parents	Abstract of Final Program Evaluation included in Parent Newsletter and PowerPoint presentation at Parent-Teacher meeting(s) at each school
School Board	Final Program Evaluation submitted as paper to members ahead of meeting to be followed up with PowerPoint presentation at School Board meeting
Curriculum Planning Committee	Handout submitted along with PowerPoint presentation at Monthly Curriculum Planning Committee meeting

FINAL THOUGHTS

Evaluation is an important part of developing a systematic understanding of what is being accomplished in schools (Stufflebeam and Shinkfield 2007) . It can help demonstrate that what we are doing works; but it is equally important as a tool to gain information that will lead to improvement. Teaching children to read and write is important for the future of our citizenry and as such, should not be taken lightly or left to chance and personal preference. The literacy curricula that schools and districts adopt must be as effective as it can be and take into account current research and recommendations for best practice.

Chapter Eight

Conclusion

You May Be Curious About . . .

To conclude, we felt as though it was necessary to address some issues that may arise while on the road to reform. Throughout the chapters, we have highlighted an actual school district that has successfully transformed the delivery of literacy instruction. We have been clear in assuring the reader that although successful in their endeavor, it was not easy.

The following are a few stumbling blocks that arose in the process of reforming literacy instruction district-wide and the creative approaches the team took to address them. Every school and district is different, yet we believe the key to the process is transparency, open-mindedness and the power of the collective. Everyone wants to teach with urgency. Everyone strives for success.

These are common goals that all conscientious educators share. No person is perfect and no program will be perfect for all, but curriculum that focuses first and foremost on the needs of the students in the seats, and holds politics secondary, is reform at its best. Success naturally falls into place.

How do a few teachers who believe in the potential of a teacher-created program that is responsive to the needs of their students, effect change in a district that is reluctant to go beyond the "security" often felt from a purchased, traditional core program?

Hopefully, after reading the previous chapters in this book, it is clear that the power to effectuate change must come from the collective, unified voices of the teachers—the boots on the ground. This requires more than a group of teachers basing their campaign for a home-grown program on the fact that they know their students better than the writers of large textbook companies, or that they teach best when they are given autonomy to teach how they want.

Necessary to their plight is evidence and research-based facts that support their desire to reform literacy instruction as it's been delivered in years past. The district that we highlighted throughout this book knew the time was right to explore reformation options and they did so with careful, methodical purpose. The drivers of the reform process took time to research recent scientific findings, observe instruction in other schools, pore over various data resources, and explore professional development via "experts" in the field, among other avenues. The stakeholders demanded such a process and the teachers rose to the occasion.

Approximately how many people should be a part of the core "design" team when writing a home-grown program?

Like any team or committee working toward change, the number of people can make or break the process. At the onset of the design process, the teachers who were interested in writing a home-grown program were plentiful. At times it appeared as if it were to the detriment of the final product; think "too many cooks in the kitchen."

However, as the team and the process evolved, some teachers stepped away from the process, others came forward, eventually creating a district literacy team that, for the most part, has remained stable for a number of years. No one was ever discouraged from joining the design team; a place was always made for them.

In a district of about four thousand students, the design team has stayed within approximately twenty to twenty-five members. During the initial design and writing process, the team met as a whole each month, while grade-level teams met on the side to work together. In its maintenance stage, the program requires tweaking and some reevaluating, but generally monthly meetings work—usually with the elementary teachers meeting separately from the middle-school teachers. The entire team comes together approximately two to three times each year. The literacy facilitators play a crucial role in coordinating and communicating program and teacher needs.

What are some options for teachers who want to write the curriculum but can't miss classroom time with their students?

There is no question that in order to undertake such an endeavor, full buy-in from the administration is essential to the process. Teachers must be given time within the school day to work on curriculum, which requires hiring substitutes to cover their classrooms. If this is not an option, teachers could be asked to work after school or during the summer months with compensation. Early release days or days usually used for workshops or in-services could also be an option. It is up to the district leaders to utilize their creativity since each school district has its own set of unique circumstances.

Are test scores the only way the stakeholders know the program is effective?

It should not be, but for many, test scores are the most popular indicator of success. Over the last few years there has been an upsurge in data teams who use numbers for a variety of reasons: to report a school's/district's yearly progress, basis for merit pay, for teacher evaluation tools, program effectiveness, and to inform and drive instruction, among others.

There is no denying that numbers show one piece of the picture but a dynamic educator and introspective administrator know better. We cannot ignore test scores but it would be irresponsible and incomplete to use only numbers as the source of our decision making.

If a home-grown program is creating passionate, engaged readers and writers, then it is doing one part of its job. If the teachers have a renewed excitement for teaching and feel empowered because they truly believe they are making a difference, fantastic, but the data cannot be ignored. When a district is committed to teaching the standards by way of a child-centered program designed by its teachers, it is up to the project managers, literacy facilitators, and teachers themselves to meet criteria set up by stakeholders.

Oftentimes, when a "hole" is discovered in the curriculum, teachers will be the first to recognize that, and they are holonomous enough to fill in that hole and make sure others have the updated information they need to properly address that standard. Other times, holes are noticed by administrators and literacy facilitators when they look at overall student achievement.

Resources and materials may need to be adjusted or supplemented, and perhaps the professional development provided may not be enough or up to par. This includes the people who provide the professional development. Do they possess the level of expertise necessary to support their teachers and administrators? Just because a person holds a title, it does not guarantee that she has the interpersonal skills needed to work well with people, train staff in research-based best practices, or even manage the requirements of the program with efficiency (e.g. data management, resource replenishment, grade-level meetings, etc.).

There will be an abundance of naysayers along the way. Creating a home-grown program can be frustrating and overwhelming at times. It is a trying endeavor that tests the core of most professionals who take part in its development. When teachers consider that they have a choice to *invest* their energy into this innovation or *spend* their energy learning how to adapt a core curriculum to their students, the choice becomes crystal clear.

The bottom line, just as in any curriculum/program, whether purchased or self-designed, is that ample time for desired results is essential. The dedication and belief that a difference can be made through the collaborative efforts of a group of educators invested in what is right for their students, is a necessary component in creating lifelong learners in addition to increasing test scores.

What if a district has sets of materials that were acquired as part of a core-program purchase?

The more materials the better! Schools should be encouraged to blend current materials into their home-grown program if they have found them to be effective in the past. Remember, a teacher-designed, home-grown literacy program provides the "what" to teachers based on the standards. Teachers infuse the program with lessons and materials that match their students' learning styles and interests while reflecting their teaching styles. In a time when budgets are being cut and resources are scarce, teachers should be encouraged to utilize what they have before purchasing new items.

An additional item to consider is professional resources for teachers. Often, most of the budget is spent on books for children, but it is of equal importance to include professional publications for teachers and administrators. This will ensure that the learning continues and the program evolves over time.

How does a literacy leader, charged with program coordination, deal with classroom teachers who are used to and enjoy the "safety" and predictability of a scripted program and do not welcome the autonomy of a home-grown program?

The bottom line here is that if the standards are driving instruction, teachers do not need to make sweeping changes. Unquestionably, they will need to restructure their instruction, to some extent, particularly if the program adoption is a district-wide initiative and purchased resources are in line with the new curriculum, or if the goal of a district-wide home-grown program is to foster continuity. Then, it is important that all teachers teach the same content, use the same instructional language, and maintaining a pace that is parallel with the grade level's classrooms.

This is essential when it comes time to assess the students and evaluate the program. The hallmark of a program that is created by the district's teachers is that it responds to the needs of the students as well as provides a collegiality that only betters the teaching in the district.

As in any profession there are mandates. Whether we like it or not, there are certain components of our job for which we are held accountable. Teachers who are reluctant to dive headfirst into a new program should be given the time to ease into it with the assistance of the literacy facilitator or, perhaps, colleagues they trust and respect. Typically, when autonomy holonomy is balanced with accountability, teachers respond positively and find that changes they are making are less painful than expected!

Isn't it just easier to buy a program already written?

Easier, yes. More effective, no. Anything that is tailored or custom made is going to fit much better, whether it be a tailor-made suit or a batch of brownies made from scratch rather than a box. We often go for the department store clothing or the packaged brownie mix because they are simply less expensive and provide a level of convenience in a fast-paced world. Both of the products mentioned are made with science behind them (test kitchens, fabric and size calibrations, etc.). But if given the opportunity, most of us would select items that were designed or created with our size, comfort, and taste in mind.

Imagine this idea with literacy instruction. Prepackaged programs are steeped in scientific research and are relatively quick to implement (although not inexpensive), but they may not match the tastes of the learners. Just like a tailor-made suit or brownies made from scratch, a home-grown, custom-designed literacy program may be labor intensive to create, but its results are well worth the effort.

It is time for teachers to find their voices in curriculum design and development and it is time for administrators, the public, and politicians to listen to those voices. When teachers' voices are heard, the future of the literacy landscape is promising for students and rewarding for teachers.

Works Cited

Allington, R. L. (20*f*02). What I've learned about effective reading instruction from a decade of studying exemplary elementary classroom teachers. *Phi Delta Kappan, 83*, 740–47.

Allington, R. L. (2001). *What really matters for struggling readers: Designing research-based programs*. New York: Longman.

Apple, M. W. (2004). *Ideology and curriculum*. London: Routledge & K. Paul.

Bandura, A. (1994). Self-efficacy. In V. S. Ramachaudran (Ed.), *Encyclopedia of human behavior* (Vol. 4, pp. 71–81). New York: Academic Press. (Reprinted in H. Friedman [Ed.], *Encyclopedia of mental health*. San Diego: Academic Press, 1998).

Bandura, A. (1977). Self-efficacy: Toward a unifying theory of behavior change, *Psychological Review, 84*, 191–215.

Bandura, A. (1986). *Social foundations of thought and action: A social cognitive theory*. Englewood Cliffs, NJ: Prentice Hall.

Beaver, Joetta. *DRA*. New Jersey: Celebration Press, Pearson Learning Group, 2001.

Beck, I. L., McKeown, M. G., & Kucan, L. (2002). *Bringing words to life: Robust vocabulary instruction*. New York: Guilford Press.

Booth, D. W., & Rowsell, J. (2002). *The literacy principal: Leading, supporting and assessing reading and writing initiatives*. Markham, Ontario, Canada: Pembroke.

Briggs-Badger, J. (2009). Executive summary, In *Dover's growing readers presentation binder*, Dover School District, Dover, NH.

Casey, K. (2006). *Literacy coaching: The essentials*. Portsmouth, NH: Heinemann.

Cserniak, C., & Schriver-Waldron, M. (1991). A study of science teaching efficacy using qualitative and quantitative research methods. Paper presented at the annual meeting of the National Association for Research in Science Teaching, April, Lake Geneva, WI.

Darling-Hammond, L. and Richardson, N. (2009). Teacher learning: What matters. *Educational Leadership, 66*(5), 46–53.

Dewey, J. (1916/1966). *Democracy and Education. An introduction to the philosophy of education*. New York: Free Press.

Dewey, J. (1938/1963). *Experience and Education*. New York: Collier Books.

Diamond, L. (2004). High Fidelity – It's not about music or marriage: It's all about instructional materials. Bay Area School ReformCollaborative. Available at http://www.corelearn.com/files/High Fidelity.pdf

Dutton, M. (1990). An investigation of the relationship between training in cooperative learning and teacher job satisfaction. Doctoral dissertation. Portland State University, Portland, OR.

Elmore, R. (2002). Bridging the Gap between Standards and Achievement The Imperative for Professional Development in Education. *Albert Shanker Institute*, 1–44. 15 Apr. 2012. http://citeseerx.ist.psu.edu.

Elmore, R. (2003). *Knowing the right thing to do: School improvement and performance-based accountability*. Washington, DC: NGA Center for Best Practices.

Fullan, M. (2007). Change the terms for teacher learning. *National Staff Development Council 28*(3) 35–36.

Gamoran, A., & Porter, A. (1994). Teacher empowerment: Can it help teaching and learning? *Educators' Notebook, 6*(2).

Gamse, B.C., Jacob, R.T., Horst, M., Boulay, B., and Unlu, F. (2008). *Reading first impact study final report executive summary* (NCEE 2009-4039). Washington, DC: National Center for Education Evaluation and Regional Assistance, Institute of Education Sciences, U.S. Department of Education.

Goddard, R. D., Hoy, W. K., & Woolfolk Hoy, A. (2000). Collective teacher efficacy: Its meaning, measure, and impact on student achievement. *American Educational Research Journal, 37*(2), 479–507.

Gutmann, A. (1987). *Democratic education*. Princeton, NJ: Princeton UP.

Hani, J., Czerniak, C., & Lumpe, A. (1996). Teacher beliefs and intentions regarding the implementation of science education reform strands. *Journal of Research in Science Teaching, 33*(9), 971–93.

Hargreaves, A. & Fullan, M. (2012). *Professional Capital*, New York: Teachers College Press.

Hargreaves, A. & Fullan, M. (1998). *What's Worth Fighting For Out There*. New York: Teachers College Press.

Hargreaves, A. et al. (eds.), *Second international handbook of educational change,* Springer International Handbooks of Education 23, DOI 10. 1007/978-90-481-2660-6_7

Harris, A. and Spillane, J. (2008). Distributed leadership through the looking glass. *Management in Education* 2008; 22; 31. DOI: 10.1177/0892020607085623

Hoy, W. K., & Tarter, C. J. (2004). Organizational justice in schools: No justice without trust. *International Journal of Educational Management, 18*, 250–59.

Hunt, Jr., (2009), Foreword in Darling-Hammond, (2009). Professional learning in the learning profession: A status report of teacher development in the United States and abroad. National Staff Development Council, Stanford University.

International Reading Association. (2004). *The role and qualifications of the reading coach in the United States. A position statement of the International Reading Association.* Newark, DE.

Ivey, G., and M. I. Baker. (2001). Phonics instruction for older students? Just say no. *Educational Leadership* 61. 35–39.

Janis, Irving L. (1982). *Groupthink: Psychological studies of policy decisions and fiascoes.* Second Edition. New York: Houghton Mifflin.

Katzenmeyer, M., and Moller, G. (1996). *Awakening the sleeping giant: Leadership development for teachers.* Thousand Oaks, CA: Corwin.

Knowles, M. S. (1970, 1980). *The modern practice of adult education: Andragogy versus pedagogy.* Englewood Cliffs: Prentice Hall/Cambridge.

Kucer, Stephen B. (2008). *What research really says about teaching and learning to read.* Urbana, IL: National Council of Teachers of English.

Lipsky, M. (1980). *Street-level bureaucracy: Dilemmas of the individual in public services.* New York: Russell Sage Foundation.

Marzano, R. J., Waters, T. & McNulty, B. A. (2005). *School leadership that works: From research to results.* Alexandria, VA: Association for Supervision and Curriculum Development.

Michael, B. & Mourshed, M. (2007) *How the world's best-performing school systems come out on top.* McKinsey & Company.

Moran, Mary Catherine. (2007). *Differentiated Literacy Coaching: Scaffolding for Student and Teacher Success.* Alexandria, VA: Association for Supervision and Curriculum Development.

National Education Commission on Time and Learning. (1994). *Prisoners of time.* Washington, DC: U.S. Government Printing Office.

Riggs, I. M., & L. G. Enochs. (1990). Toward the development of an elementary teacher's science teaching efficacy belief instrument. *Science Education, 74*(6), 625–37.

Ross, J. A. (1992). Teacher Efficacy and the effect of coaching on student achievement. *Canadian Journal of Education, 17*(1), 51–65.

Routman, R. (2003). *Reading Essentials: The Specifics You Need to Teach Reading Well.* Portsmouth, NH: Heinemann.

Senge, P. M. (1999). *The dance of change: The challenges of sustaining momentum in learning organizations.* New York: Currency/Doubleday.

Stufflebeam, D. L., & Shinkfield, A. J. (2007). *Evaluation theory, models, and applications.* San Francisco: Jossey-Bass

Vygotsky, L. (1978). Interaction between Learning and Development (pp. 79–91). In *Mind in Society.* (Trans. M. Cole). Cambridge, MA: Harvard University Press.